# minutemeals

# quick &
# healthy

### delicious, good-for-you dinners

Edited by Miriam Garron

Wiley Publishing, Inc.

Library of Congress Cataloging-in-Publication Data

Minutemeals quick & healthy : delicious good-for-you dinners / edited by Miriam Garron.
    p. cm.
  ISBN 0-7645-1773-2
  1. Quick and easy cookery. 2. Menus. I. Title: Minutemeals quick and healthy. II. Garron, Miriam.
  TX833.5 .M56 2003
  641.5'55—dc21                                                                  2002013837

minutemeals

Joe Langhan, President, MinuteMeals.com, Inc.
Cathy Wallach, Director of Marketing and Public Relations
Miriam Garron, Managing Editor
Miriam Rubin, Consulting Food Editor
Cover design by Edwin Kuo
Interior design by Edwin Kuo
Cover photograph by David Bishop

Manufactured in China

10 9 8 7 6 5 4 3 2 1

# welcome to *minutemeals quick & healthy*,

the fifth volume in the minutemeals series of cookbooks. If you are a visitor to our website, minutemeals.com, or own any of the previous minutemeals cookbooks, you know that our 20-minute menus are the keys to easy, delectable family dinners. If you are a minutemeals novice, what better way to jump-start the family dinnertime than with great, easy meals that are good for you, too?

**here's what you can expect** from the "quick" part of *minutemeals quick & healthy.* As always, the menus include complete meals, including dessert, that go from counter to table in 20 minutes or less, shopping and pantry lists, an "at-a-glance" gameplan of the steps in the menu, and useful tips from our professional chefs.

**and the healthy?** It's what you urged us to do in hundreds of emails to the site: Limit the amount of saturated fat, cholesterol, and sodium, and control the calorie count. So that's what we did. *minutemeals quick & healthy* menus are not "diet" menus, nor menus designed to meet specific medical needs, but delicious, satisfying meals based on recognized guidelines for a healthy, balanced diet. Here's what "healthy" means at minutemeals:

**in accordance with the USDA** definition of "low-fat," our menus contain no more than 30% of calories from fat.

**we allowed for** 750 nutrient-rich calories for the whole meal, including dessert, to provide a filling yet nutritious meal for each member of the family. Many of the menus fall well below that ceiling. The National Academy of Sciences/USDA daily calorie intake recommendations range from 1600 to 2800 calories, depending on age, activity level, and gender. Food producers use a daily calorie intake of 2000 when calculating percentages of nutrients for package labels.

**taking our cue** from the latest dietary guidelines of both the American Heart Association (AHA) and the USDA, our menus emphasize vegetables, fruits, and grains, include low-fat meats and dairy products, and limit saturated fat, cholesterol, and high calorie and/or low nutrient foods.

**again following the lead** of the AHA, which recommends consuming no more than 300mg of cholesterol and 2400mg of sodium per day, our menus generally include no more than 100mg of cholesterol and 1000mg of sodium.

**the 80 menus that follow** offer everything you love about minutemeals: easy-to-find ingredients, scrupulously organized instructions, delicious recipes—and less. Less fat, less sodium, less cholesterol. Less anxiety, too. We've crunched the numbers so you don't have to—choose any menu in the book and rest assured that your family will be soon be savoring a balanced, nutritious meal. So from the chefs at minutemeals—to your health!

Miriam Garron, *Editor*

# minutemeals
## quick
## & healthy

# meet the minutemeals chefs

We'd like you to meet the chefs behind minutemeals, the people whose creativity and ingenuity created the delicious menus in this book. Their combined expertise is our ace in the hole—the secret that keeps our menus fresh, interesting, and full of great ideas. You'll find their helpful comments throughout the book, paired with the menus they created.

David Bonom

Lisa Cherkasky

Hillary Davis-Tonken

Ruth Fisher

Wendy Kalen

Marge Perry

Paul E. Piccuito

Sarah Reynolds

Patty Santelli

# how to use this book

**minutemeals quick & healthy** is designed to be as efficient as possible. Twenty minutes, after all, is a short amount of time to cook a full meal and place it on the table. For you to be able to do the cooking with as few setbacks as possible, we took care of as many of the time-consuming details as we could to insure your success.

Each menu includes a shopping list of the major ingredients needed, as well as a complete list of ingredients we consider standard pantry items. No more hunting through multiple recipes to glean what you need to buy on the way home—we've done that for you. Our "menu gameplan" then orders the sequence of just how to go about cooking the meal—what dish needs to be started first, what should follow, and so on. We've

also noted when to preheat the oven or broiler so that it will be sufficiently heated for maximum cooking results, and when you need to put water on to boil for pasta and rice. The double-page format of each menu guarantees that when you refer to the cooking directions of any given dish you are always on the "same page."

The minutemeals clock starts ticking when you put the ingredients for a menu on the kitchen counter. The first several times you make a menu expect it to take a few minutes more than you had anticipated: The system itself and the recipes are new to you and, as the saying goes, practice makes perfect.

As in all of our cookbooks, the 80 menus in *minutemeals quick & healthy* end with a nutritional analysis. However, for this book we gave you an analysis of the whole menu, not just the main dish as we usually do. If you have particular dietary concerns or preferences, please check the numbers before you choose your menu. Does one of our Asian-inspired menus, say, contain just a bit more sodium than you'd like? Browse a bit—we're confident that you'll find many other menus that meet your needs. Choose from a variety of quick, easy, healthy, delicious menus—what more could you possibly want?

# quick tips from the pros

## michel nischan

### the soy of cooking

**tofu is just the tip of the soy iceberg.** Try these simple tips for adding soy protein to your diet:

**fresh-frozen soybeans (edamame):** I use them, straight from the freezer, in place of lima beans in succotash. Or I boil them 4 minutes, salt them and serve them as a nosh; boiled a bit longer and pureed with silken tofu and blanched garlic, they make a terrific dip.

**miso paste:** Used in place of salt, it also gives a slightly sweet, smoky note to seasoning rubs, marinades, and sauces. My favorite quick sauce is a combination of soy sauce, chicken broth, lemon juice, grated fresh ginger, a touch of miso, and chopped scallions.

**tofu:** Tofu-avoidance can be cured by using the right tofu for the right dish. Here's a primer: Firm tofu should be sliced, drained on a dry towel until all the liquid drains out, then marinated and grilled. Soft tofu can be used in soups and stir-fries, or battered and fried. Silken tofu should be sliced with a sharp knife, marinated in tamari with some raw sugar, then seared under a hot broiler until well browned—the resulting texture is similar to that of a hot custard. Silken tofu is also a healthy substitute for sour cream or mayonnaise in dips and spreads.

Michel Nischan is the Executive Chef at New York City's renowned Heartbeat, which features healthful dishes using whole, natural foods and no butter or heavy dairy products. Michel previously owned restaurants in Connecticut and Wisconsin, where he started his culinary career as a breakfast cook. He appears regularly on cable television's Food Network, is a Contributing Authority to Food Arts magazine, and also contributes to a variety of magazines and newspapers. He is on the board of The Chefs Collaborative, which promotes sustainable agriculture and cuisine, a key organizer of the New American Farming Initiative, and a member of the Founders Committee for the Amazon Conservation Team. His first cookbook will be published by Chronicle Books in 2003.

# david poran

## comfort food without the fat

**as Executive Chef of the National Football League, I cook for a very health-conscious bunch of eaters.** I've worked hard to develop simple methods that allow me to cook their favorite comfort foods but with far less fat:

**crank up the heat:** One of the most popular vegetables at NFL headquarters is roasted caramelized cauliflower. Caramelizing—browning their natural sugars—works for most vegetables with a low water content, like carrots, winter squash, baby onions, and potatoes. The 3 most important things to keep in mind when caramelizing: Use just enough olive oil to lightly coat the vegetable pieces, don't crowd the pieces in the roasting pan, and DON'T FEAR THE HEAT! Crank up your oven to 500°F or even 550°F. To caramelize cauliflower, toss 1 head, broken into small florets, with 2 tablespoons olive oil and salt and pepper to taste, and roast for just 10 minutes or so.

**fry food—without frying:** You can't argue with the great things that happen to food when it is fried, and you can get the same results from oven roasting: Bread a piece of chicken or fish with flour, egg, and breadcrumbs as you normally would, and place it on a cookie sheet sprayed with olive oil spray. Mist the top of the food with a generous amount of spray—the mist lets you coat everything well without actually using much oil. Bake at 400°F–425°F until golden-browned and crisp.

David Poran is the Executive Chef of the National Football League. An honors graduate of the Culinary Institute of America, David worked with renowned chef Daniel Boulud. David then worked as a saucier at Manhattan's Rhiga Royal Hotel before taking on the role of Executive Chef at a small and well-received restaurant on Manhattan's Upper West Side. After subsequent stints at Goldman Sachs and as a freelance consultant, David took the position he now holds with the NFL.

# bill boggs

## dining in—keeping the fat out

**i make my living dining out on rich foods and spectacular desserts.** So I've had to hone some techniques that keep my home cooking as light and quick as possible:

**i cook virtually everything in nonstick skillets with ovenproof handles:** I just heat the skillet until it is very hot, then, without adding fat, I sear lean meat like buffalo or ostrich—steaks or ground—and then pop the pan into the oven briefly to finish the cooking. I have skillets of various sizes so that I can cook a burger or a large roast.

**i keep homemade, fat-free sauces and marinades on hand to add flavor and moisture to lean meats:** A mixture of Dijon mustard and horseradish is my favorite sauce for chicken breasts. I roast the breasts at 350°F with a spritz of fresh lemon juice, let them cool briefly, and then smear them with the sauce. My standby marinade for pork tenderloin is a combination orange and pineapple juices, balsamic vinegar, and fresh garlic. I marinate the meat, sear it in the nonstick skillet, and then roast it briefly, adding a bit of marinade to the pan toward the end of the roasting time to create a nice pan sauce.

**i rely on organic ingredients:** Organic vegetables and meat are so flavorful, I find I don't need to gussy them up. Steamed organic vegetables with salt and pepper are terrific with any meal.

As the host of Food Television's Bill Boggs Corner Table, Daily Dish, and Food Network Live, and as a prolific contributor to magazines and newspapers, Bill Boggs has interviewed hundreds of chefs, restaurateurs, and cookbook authors. Bill is currently the restaurant critic for Black Tie magazine, and is writing a book on aging, diet, and lifestyle. Bill is a 4-time Emmy winning television host and produces television programs as well.

minute

quick

# soups and salads

meals
& healthy

# chicken waldorf salad
## with apples and grapes
### wasa crisp breads
### fresh cherries and chocolate biscotti

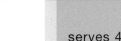

## menu
## gameplan

## shopping list

Skinless boneless chicken breasts

Gala or Golden Delicious apple

Red seedless grapes (from the salad bar)

Red onion slices (from the salad bar)

Celery

Plain low-fat yogurt

Frozen apple juice concentrate

Chopped walnuts

Wasa Crisp Breads

Chocolate biscotti

Cherries

## from your pantry

Salt

Low-fat mayonnaise

Freshly ground black pepper

serves 4

## beforeyoustart

Bring the water to a boil in a large, deep skillet, covered, over high heat, to cook the chicken. Rinse and chill the cherries.

step 1 prepare the **chicken waldorf salad with apples and grapes**

step 2 **serve**

## luckyforyou

If you are really crunched for time, you can prepare the salad with the packaged sliced, precooked chicken available in the poultry case at most supermarkets. Remember, though, that the packaged precooked chicken will contain sodium.

*"This creamy, colorful salad proves that a retro classic can be healthy, too."*

—minutemeals' Chef Hillary

## prepare the **chicken waldorf salad with apples and grapes**

4 cups water

Salt to taste

8 ounces skinless boneless chicken breasts

1 large Gala or Golden Delicious apple

1 celery stalk

1 cup red seedless grapes

$1/2$ cup red onion slices

$1/4$ cup low-fat mayonnaise

$1/4$ cup plain low-fat yogurt

1 tablespoon frozen apple juice concentrate

Salt and freshly ground black pepper to taste

2 tablespoons chopped walnuts

1. In a large deep skillet, bring 1 inch of water to a boil, covered, over high heat. Add the salt and the chicken. Reduce the heat to low, cover, and simmer 5 to 8 minutes, until the chicken is just cooked through. Transfer the chicken to a plate until cool enough to handle.

2. While the chicken cooks, cut the apple into $1/2$-inch pieces. Thinly slice the celery on the diagonal, and halve the grapes. Coarsely chop the red onion slices.

3. When the chicken is cool enough to handle, cut it into small pieces. In a salad bowl, stir together the mayonnaise, yogurt, and apple juice. Add the chicken, apple, celery, grapes, red onion, and salt and pepper to the mayonnaise mixture and stir to mix well.

## serve

1. Divide the salad among 4 large plates. Sprinkle each portion with some of the chopped walnuts, dividing evenly. Arrange pieces of Wasa crisp bread at the edge of each salad.

2. When ready for dessert, serve 2 chocolate biscotti and $1/2$ cup cherries per person.

---

**Chicken Waldorf Salad with Apples and Grapes**
Single serving is $1/4$ of the total menu

CALORIES 436; PROTEIN 23g; CARBS 58g; TOTAL FAT 14g; SAT FAT 4g; CHOLESTEROL 70mg; SODIUM 604mg; FIBER 7g

*28% of calories from fat*

# corn, tomato, and avocado salad
## with smoked turkey
### speedy gazpacho
### breadsticks
### peach halves with amaretti

menu
**game**plan

## shopping list

Frozen corn kernels

Smoked turkey
(from the deli counter)

Scallions

Fresh cilantro

Vine-ripe tomato

Ripe avocado

Lime (for juice)

Reduced-fat red wine
vinaigrette dressing

Romaine lettuce

Seedless cucumber

Radishes

Low-sodium mixed vegetable
juice

Ripe peaches

Amaretti cookies

Sliced almonds

Breadsticks

## from your pantry

Pepper

Mild Louisiana-style cayenne
pepper sauce

Red wine vinegar

serves 4

## **before**youstart

Place the mixed vegetable juice in the
freezer to quickly chill.

step **1** make the **corn, tomato, and avocado salad with smoked turkey**

step **2** make the **speedy gazpacho**

step **3** prepare the **peach halves with amaretti**

step **4** **serve**

## headsup

To easily dice an avocado, cut
the avocado in half and remove
the pit. Hold one half, cut side up, on a kitchen towel in
your palm. Using a paring knife, make parallel slices. Turn
the avocado 90 degrees and repeat. Scoop out the diced
avocado with a tablespoon. Repeat with the other half.

*"This menu makes no demands on your supermarket. Every ingredient here is easy to find."*

—minutemeals' Chef Paul

## step 1

### make the **corn, tomato, and avocado salad with smoked turkey**

1 package (16 ounces) frozen corn kernels

1 chunk (8 ounces) smoked turkey

2 scallions

2 tablespoons chopped cilantro

1 medium vine-ripe tomato

1 ripe avocado

1 lime

1/4 cup quality reduced-fat red wine vinaigrette dressing

Pepper to taste

8 crispy romaine lettuce leaves (from the inside of the head)

**1.** Cook the corn in a microwave-safe container, according to the directions on the package. Drain the cooked corn in a sieve, rinse with cold running water, drain again, and place in a medium serving bowl.

**2.** Cut the turkey into 3/4-inch cubes and add to the corn. Thinly slice the scallions and chop the cilantro; add to the bowl. Dice the tomato; halve, pit, and dice the avocado; add to the bowl. Squeeze the lime to get 1 1/2 tablespoons juice. Add the lime juice and vinaigrette dressing into the corn and turkey mixture, and toss to coat. Season with pepper.

## step 2

### make the **speedy gazpacho**

4-inch length of seedless cucumber

3 scallions

6 radishes

2 1/2 cups low-sodium mixed vegetable juice

1 tablespoon mild Louisiana-style cayenne pepper sauce

2 teaspoons red wine vinegar

Cut the cucumber and scallions into 2-inch chunks; cut the radishes in half; place in a blender. Add the vegetable juice, pepper sauce, and vinegar to the blender and process until finely chopped.

## step 3

### prepare the **peach halves with amaretti**

4 ripe peaches

8 amaretti cookies (1 1/4 ounces)

1 tablespoon sliced almonds

**1.** Cut the peaches in half, remove the pits and reassemble, to keep the flesh from browning.

**2.** Place the amaretti and the almonds in small plastic bag and, using your palm, coarsely crush the mixture until the amaretti are in 1/4-inch pieces.

## step 4

### serve

**1.** Place 2 romaine lettuce leaves on each of 4 dinner plates. Mound the salad on the plates, dividing evenly.

**2.** Pour the gazpacho into bowls or mugs and serve with the salad. Pass the breadsticks, allowing 2 per person.

**3.** When ready for dessert, open the peaches and place 2 halves, cut side up, on each of 4 small plates. Sprinkle the amaretti/almond mixture evenly over the tops and serve.

---

**Corn, Tomato, and Avocado Salad with Smoked Turkey**
Single serving is 1/4 of the total menu
CALORIES 511; PROTEIN 21g; CARBS 80g;
TOTAL FAT 16g; SAT FAT 3g; CHOLESTEROL 24mg;
SODIUM 991mg; FIBER 14g
*26% of calories from fat*

# grilled salmon caesar salad

## breadsticks

## watermelon and grape medley with biscotti

## menu
## gameplan

### shopping list

Biscotti

Salmon fillets

Lemon (for zest and juice)

Prewashed romaine salad greens

Grape tomatoes

Low-fat herb or Caesar-flavored packaged croutons

Breadsticks

### from the salad bar

Seedless red and/or green grapes

Seedless watermelon chunks

Cucumber slices

### from your pantry

Honey

Vegetable cooking spray

Salt

Freshly ground black pepper

Fat-free reduced-sodium chicken broth or vegetable

Garlic

Low-fat mayonnaise

Grated Parmesan cheese

serves 4

### beforeyoustart

Rinse and chill the grapes for dessert.

step 1 prepare the **watermelon and grape medley**

step 2 prepare the **grilled salmon caesar salad**

step 3 **serve**

## headsup

We call for peeling strips of zest from the lemon here, instead of grating it, because most people just don't have a grater that handles the task efficiently. Use a light hand and peel only the zest—the thin, yellow outer membrane of the lemon—not the bitter white pith underneath.

*"Caesar salad has become so popular, I knew it was the right time for this healthy, main-dish version."*

—minutemeals' Chef Paul

## step 1

### prepare the **watermelon and grape medley with biscotti**

8 ounces seedless red and/or green grapes

1 1/2 cups seedless watermelon chunks

2 tablespoons honey

4 biscotti, for serving

Rinse and dry the grapes. Place the grapes and the watermelon chunks in a medium bowl. Add the honey and toss to combine.

## step 2

### prepare the **grilled salmon caesar salad**

**for the salmon**

Vegetable cooking spray

4 salmon fillets, each 4 ounces

Salt and pepper to taste

**for the dressing**

2 garlic cloves, peeled and flattened with a knife blade

1/3 cup fat-free reduced-sodium chicken or vegetable broth

1 lemon, scrubbed

3 tablespoons low-fat mayonnaise

1/4 cup grated Parmesan cheese

Freshly ground pepper to taste

1 bag (5 ounces) prewashed romaine salad greens

1 cup grape tomatoes

1 cup cucumber slices

1 cup low-fat herb or Caesar-flavored packaged croutons

1. Spray a grill pan with vegetable cooking spray. Place the pan over medium heat. Season the salmon on both sides with salt and pepper. Add the salmon to the pan and cook for about 8 minutes, turning halfway during the cooking, until done in the center.

2. Meanwhile, place the garlic and broth in a small dish. Cover with plastic wrap and microwave on High for 45 to 60 seconds, or until the garlic is tender when pierced with a knife. Using a vegetable peeler, peel two wide strips of zest from the lemon, being careful to get just the yellow part of the peel, not the white underneath (the pith). Halve the lemon and squeeze enough juice to measure 1 tablespoon.

3. Place the garlic, lemon zest and juice, mayonnaise, 2 tablespoons of the Parmesan cheese, and pepper in a mini-processor or blender. Blend until smooth.

4. Place the greens, grape tomatoes, and cucumber slices in a large salad bowl. Toss with the dressing.

## step 3

### serve

1. Divide the salad among 4 dinner plates. Scatter the croutons on top of the greens.

2. Top each salad with a salmon fillet, and sprinkle the remaining 2 tablespoons Parmesan cheese over the tops, dividing evenly. Serve the salads with the breadsticks, allowing 2 breadsticks per person.

3. When ready for dessert, toss the fruit mixture again, spoon into dessert dishes and serve with the biscotti.

Grilled Salmon Caesar Salad
Single serving is 1/4 of the total menu
CALORIES 439; PROTEIN 28g; CARBS 55g;
TOTAL FAT 12g; SAT FAT 4g; CHOLESTEROL 86mg;
SODIUM 726mg; FIBER 4g
*25% of calories from fat*

# caribbean shrimp salad
## with curried pineapple dressing
### spiced pita chips
### chocolate sorbet with raspberries

## shopping list

Pita breads (6-inch diameter)

Mango

Precut cantaloupe chunks

Jalapeño pepper

Red onion slices
(from the salad bar)

Canned juice-packed
pineapple

Large shrimp, cooked,
peeled, and deveined

Fresh cilantro

Raspberries (2 cups)

Chocolate sorbet (2 cups)

## from your pantry

Olive oil

Paprika

Ground coriander

Salt

Freshly ground black pepper

Rice vinegar

Curry powder

serves 4

## **before**youstart

Preheat the oven to 425°F to toast the pita chips.

| step | 1 | make the **spiced pita chips** |
| step | 2 | assemble the **shrimp salad** |
| step | 3 | **serve** |

 We borrowed one of the great innovations of nouvelle cuisine here by using fruit juice and purée to create a salad dressing that's flavorful and creamy, but without a drop of fat.

*"I balanced sweet with spicy in this salad. If you want to tip the balance toward spicy, try hot curry powder."*

—minutemeals' Chef David

## step 1

### make the **spiced pita chips**

4 pita breads (6-inch diameter)

1 tablespoon olive oil

2 teaspoons paprika

1 1/2 teaspoons ground coriander

Salt and freshly ground black pepper to taste

1. Preheat the oven to 425°F.

2. Brush each pita bread with some of the olive oil. Sprinkle with the paprika, coriander, salt, and pepper. Stack the pita breads and cut them into 8 triangles, making 32 wedges.

3. Arrange the pita wedges, spices side up, on a large baking sheet. Bake 7 to 10 minutes, until crisp. Remove from the oven and let cool.

## step 2

### assemble the **caribbean shrimp salad with curried pineapple dressing**

1 mango

8 ounces precut cantaloupe chunks

1 small jalapeño pepper, seeded, veins removed, and diced

1/2 cup red onion slices

2 cans (8-ounces each) pineapple chunks in juice

1 pound large shrimp, cooked, peeled and deveined

1 tablespoon rice vinegar

2 tablespoons cilantro leaves

1/2 teaspoon curry powder

Salt and freshly ground black pepper to taste

1. Peel the mango with a vegetable peeler, and slice the fruit off the pit. Cut the flesh into cubes. Coarsely chop the cantaloupe chunks. Seed, remove the veins from, and dice the jalapeño pepper; chop the red onion slices.

2. Drain 1 can of the pineapple chunks. In a large salad bowl, mix the drained pineapple with the mango, canteloupe, red onion, jalapeño pepper, and shrimp.

3. Drain the remaining can of pineapple chunks, reserving 1 tablespoon of juice. Place the pineapple, reserved juice, and the rice vinegar in a blender or food processor. Blend until smooth; add the cilantro and curry powder and pulse to chop coarsely. Pour the dressing over the shrimp and mango mixture and toss well to coat. Season with salt and pepper.

## step 3

### serve

1. Divide the shrimp salad among 4 dinner plates and bring the plates to the table.

2. Transfer the pita chips to a basket and serve with the salad.

3. When ready for dessert, divide the raspberries among 4 dessert dishes and scoop 1/2 cup of chocolate sorbet on top of each serving. Serve immediately.

---

**Caribbean Shrimp Salad with Curried Pineapple Dressing**
Single serving is 1/4 of the total menu
CALORIES 508; PROTEIN 24g; CARBS 92g;
TOTAL FAT 6g; SAT FAT 1g; CHOLESTEROL 135mg;
SODIUM 846mg; FIBER 11g
*10% of calories from fat*

# corn and crab salad

## in chili-tortillas

### sliced tomato and cucumber platter

### strawberry and pineapple fondue

menu
**game**plan

serves 4

## **before**youstart

Preheat the oven to 350°F to warm the tortillas.

| | | |
|---|---|---|
| step | 1 | make the **chili-tortillas** |
| step | 2 | assemble the **corn and crab salad** |
| step | 3 | arrange the **sliced tomato and cucumber platter** |
| step | 4 | assemble the **strawberry and pineapple fondue** |
| step | 5 | **serve** |

### shopping list

Corn tortillas
(5-inch diameter)

Canned crabmeat

Lime (for juice)

Fresh cilantro

Avocado

Corn and black bean salsa

Pre-shredded iceberg lettuce

Ripe tomatoes

White chocolate raspberry
fat-free yogurt

### From the salad bar

Cucumber slices (or from the
produce department)

Hulled or trimmed strawberries
(or from the produce
department)

Pineapple chunks

### from your pantry

Olive oil cooking spray

Chili powder

Low-fat mayonnaise

Extra virgin olive oil

Red wine vinegar

Salt and pepper

**heads**up Using vegetable spray is a good way to cut calories—the spray mechanism makes it possible to coat a pan or an ingredient lightly, evenly, and quickly. To save yourself cleanup time here, place foil on the baking sheet before you spray the tortillas, so you don't film the pan with oil.

*"Even a simple meal can include surprises. Nobody expects to find crab in tortillas, but everybody loves the combination."* —minutemeals' Chef Wendy

## step 1

### make the **chili-tortillas**

8 corn tortillas (5-inch diameter)

Olive oil cooking spray

1/2 teaspoon chili powder

1. Preheat the oven to 350°F.

2. Place the tortillas on a baking sheet. Spray lightly with olive oil cooking spray and sprinkle with chili powder. Cover the pan with aluminum foil and bake 10 minutes, until heated. Remove from the oven and keep warm until serving.

## step 2

### assemble the **corn and crab salad and garnishes**

**for the crab salad**

2 cans (6 ounces each) crabmeat

1 lime

2 tablespoons chopped cilantro

1/4 cup low-fat mayonnaise

**for the garnishes**

1 avocado

1/2 cup corn and black bean salsa

2 cups pre-shredded iceberg lettuce

1. Make the crab salad: Drain the crabmeat and place in a small bowl. Pick through the meat to remove any cartilage pieces.

2. Squeeze 1 tablespoon of juice from the lime. Chop enough cilantro to measure 2 tablespoons. In a small bowl, combine the crabmeat with the mayonnaise, lime juice, and cilantro.

3. Prepare the garnishes: Halve, pit, and dice the avocado. Place the avocado chunks, the corn and bean salsa, and the shredded lettuce in separate bowls.

4. Place the crab salad and the garnishes on the table.

## step 3

### arrange the **sliced tomato and cucumber platter**

2 large ripe tomatoes, sliced

2 cups cucumber slices

1 tablespoon extra virgin olive oil

2 teaspoons red wine vinegar

Salt and pepper to taste

Slice the tomatoes. Arrange the tomato slices, slightly overlapping, on one side of a large plate, and the cucumber slices, slightly overlapping, on the other side. Sprinkle the olive oil and red wine vinegar over the vegetables and season with salt and pepper. Set the platter on the table.

## step 4

### assemble the **strawberry and pineapple fondue**

1 container (8 ounces) white chocolate raspberry fat-free yogurt

1 cup cleaned and trimmed strawberries

1 cup fresh pineapple chunks

Transfer the yogurt to a small bowl and set on a platter. Arrange the strawberries and pineapple chunks around the yogurt, and chill until ready for dessert.

## step 5

### serve

1. Bring the warm chili-tortillas to the table. Let each diner construct 2 tortillas: Spoon 1/8 of the crab salad on 1/2 of a tortilla. Top with some of the salsa, avocado, and shredded lettuce. Roll up the tortillas. Pass the platter of tomatoes and cucumbers.

2. When ready for dessert, place the fruit and yogurt on the table and let diners dip pieces of fruit into the yogurt.

Corn and Crab Salad in Chili-Tortillas
Single serving is 1/4 of the total menu
CALORIES 426; PROTEIN 22g; CARBS 61g;
TOTAL FAT 14g; SAT FAT 2g; CHOLESTEROL 62mg;
SODIUM 679mg; FIBER 11g

*30% of calories from fat*

# tomato and chickpea salad
## with tzatziki dressing
### not-so-devilish eggs
### toasted seven-grain bread
### melon wedges with lime

## shopping list

Peeled hard-cooked eggs
(from the salad bar)

Fresh chives

Plain fat-free yogurt

Ripe tomatoes

Canned chickpeas

Sweet white onion

Kirby cucumber

Seven-grain bread

Ripe cantaloupe or
honeydew melon

Lime

## from your pantry

Reduced-fat mayonnaise

Dill-pickle relish

Grainy Dijon mustard

Salt

Freshly ground black pepper

Garlic

Extra virgin olive oil

serves 4

## beforeyoustart
Drain the yogurt for the tzatziki dressing.
(See step 2)

| step | 1 | make the **not-so-devilish eggs** |
| step | 2 | make the **tomato and chickpea salad with tzatziki dressing** |
| step | 3 | make the **toasted seven-grain bread** |
| step | 4 | prepare the **melon wedges with lime** |
| step | 5 | **serve** |

## luckyforyou
A box grater is perfect for "mincing" garlic. Be sure to use the smallest wholes on the grater. Here's another trick we've used for years: To squeeze as much liquid as possible from grated cucumber or potato, put it in the toe of clean nylon stockings and wring. (If you don't have stockings on hand, use a clean dish towel or cheesecloth.)

*"Deviled eggs look so sunny arranged on a platter. That's what inspired me to create this summery menu."*

—minutemeals' Chef Hillary

## make the **not-so-devilish eggs**

4 peeled hard-cooked eggs

2 tablespoons reduced-fat mayonnaise

2 teaspoons dill-pickle relish

1/2 teaspoon grainy Dijon mustard

1/8 teaspoon each salt and freshly ground black pepper

2 tablespoons snipped fresh chives

1. Halve the eggs lengthwise. Remove the yolks and place in a small bowl; place the whites on a plate. Using a fork, mash the yolks with the mayonnaise, relish, mustard, salt, and pepper and beat until creamy. Snip enough chives to measure 2 tablespoons. Stir 1 tablespoon into the egg yolk mixture.

2. Spoon the yolks mixture into the egg whites and sprinkle the stuffed eggs with the remaining 1 tablespoon of chives.

## make the **tomato and chickpea salad with tzatziki dressing**

1 container (8 ounces) plain fat-free yogurt

2 pounds red, ripe tomatoes

1 can (15 to 16 ounces) chickpeas, rinsed and drained

1/2 medium sweet white onion

1 medium Kirby cucumber

1 small garlic clove

1 tablespoon extra virgin olive oil

1/4 teaspoon salt

1/2 teaspoon freshly ground black pepper

1. Line a small strainer with a double layer of paper towel. Spoon the yogurt into the filter or strainer and suspend over a cup or bowl. Let yogurt drain for 10 minutes.

2. Meanwhile, core the tomatoes and cut into wedges. Arrange in a salad bowl. Drain and rinse the chickpeas, and thinly slice the onion. Sprinkle the chickpeas and the onion over the tomatoes.

3. Grate the cucumber and squeeze out the excess moisture. Place the cucumber in a small bowl. Finely grate enough garlic to measure about 1/2 teaspoon and add to the cucumber. Add the olive oil, drained yogurt, and the salt and pepper and stir to mix well.

4. Spoon the dressing over the salad and toss gently to mix.

## make the **toasted seven-grain bread**

4 slices seven-grain bread

Lightly toast the bread in the toaster or toaster oven; halve each slice diagonally, place on a plate, and cover with a napkin to keep warm.

## prepare the **melon wedges with lime**

1 ripe cantaloupe or honeydew melon

1 lime, cut into wedges

Cut the melon in half and scoop out and discard the seeds. Halve the halves, and place a melon wedge on each of 4 dessert dishes. Cut the lime into wedges and add a wedge to each plate. Chill until ready to serve dessert.

## serve

1. Place the eggs and toast on the table and serve with the tomato and chickpea salad.

2. When ready for dessert, serve the melon wedges.

---

**Tomato and Chickpea Salad with Tzatziki Dressing**
Single serving is 1/4 of the total menu
CALORIES 402; PROTEIN 19g; CARBS 58g; TOTAL FAT 14g; SAT FAT 3g; CHOLESTEROL 216mg; SODIUM 649mg; FIBER 11g
*29% of calories from fat*

# greek pasta salad

warm pita breads with
cannellini butter

plums with lemon yogurt

## shopping list

Orzo

Grape or cherry tomatoes

Kalamata olives

Reduced-fat feta cheese

Low-fat Italian dressing

Canned cannellini beans

Fresh mint

Whole-wheat pita breads
(6-inch diameter)

Plums

Lemon fat-free yogurt

### from the salad bar

Red onion slices

Cucumber slices

Prewashed spinach leaves

## from your pantry

Ground cumin

Turmeric

Kosher salt

Pepper

Ground cinnamon

serves 4

## beforeyoustart

Bring the water to a boil in a large
saucepan, covered, over high heat.

step **1** make the **greek pasta salad**

step **2** make the **cannellini butter**

step **3** prepare the **warm pita breads**

step **4** make the **plums with lemon yogurt**

step **5** **serve**

## luckyforyou

A wide variety of high-quality,
imported pitted olives are
available now in good supermarkets and specialty stores.
Search them out—you'll never go back to canned.

*"Salad and pasta in one dish—now that's convenience food. Kids especially love the orzo."*

—minutemeals' Chef Patty

## step 1
### make the **greek pasta salad**

$^1/_2$ cup orzo

1 pint grape or cherry tomatoes

$^1/_2$ cup red onion slices

12 pitted kalamata olives, chopped

3 ounces reduced-fat feta cheese, cut into small pieces

2 cups cucumber slices

$^1/_4$ cup low-fat Italian dressing

4 cups prewashed spinach leaves, torn into pieces, for serving

1. Bring a large pot of water to a boil, covered, over high heat. Add the orzo and cook according to the directions on the package until *al dente*. Drain in a fine-mesh strainer and rinse under cold running water.

2. Halve the tomatoes. Coarsely chop the red onion and the olives. Cut the feta cheese into small pieces.

3. Combine the tomatoes, cucumber slices, feta cheese, onions, olives, and orzo in a salad bowl. Add the dressing and toss gently until coated. Place the bowl on the table.

## step 2
### make the **cannellini butter**

1 can (15 ounces) cannellini beans, drained and rinsed

1 tablespoon chopped fresh mint

$^1/_2$ teaspoon ground cumin

$^1/_4$ teaspoon turmeric

$^1/_8$ teaspoon kosher salt

$^1/_8$ teaspoon pepper

1. Drain and rinse the cannellini beans. Chop enough mint to measure 1 tablespoon. Process the beans in a mini food processor or blender until creamy.

2. Add the cumin, turmeric, kosher salt, and pepper and process until well blended. Scrape the purée into a small serving bowl and stir in the mint.

## step 3
### prepare the **warm pita breads**

4 whole-wheat pita breads (6-inch diameter)

In the toaster oven, warm the pitas until heated through. Cut each pita into quarters, and place in a bread basket. Cover with a napkin to keep warm.

## step 4
### make the **plums with lemon yogurt**

6 ripe plums or 2 cans ($15^1/_4$ ounces each) plums packed in juice or water

1 container (8 ounces) lemon fat-free yogurt

Ground cinnamon

Rinse and slice the fresh plums, or drain the canned. Divide among 4 dessert dishes. Top each serving with $^1/_4$ of the lemon yogurt and a sprinkle of cinnamon. Chill until ready for dessert.

## step 5
### serve

1. Arrange 1 cup of spinach on each of 4 dinner plates. Mound the orzo salad in the center (about $1^1/_2$ cups salad per serving).

2. Place the warm pita bread on the table with cannellini butter.

3. When ready for dessert, serve the plums with yogurt.

---

**Greek Pasta Salad**
Single serving is $^1/_4$ of the total menu

CALORIES 560; PROTEIN 23g; CARBS 95g; TOTAL FAT 12g; SAT FAT 3g; CHOLESTEROL 9mg; SODIUM 1056mg; FIBER 12g

*18% of calories from fat*

# asian tofu salad
## miso soup
## mini rice cakes
## broiled bananas with chocolate sorbet

### shopping list

Orange marmalade

Snow peas (from the salad bar)

Scallions

Firm tofu

Matchstick-cut carrots (from the produce department)

Prewashed baby spinach

Miso soup mix

Ripe bananas

Chocolate sorbet

Unsalted mini rice cakes

### from your pantry

Ground ginger

Lite soy sauce

Rice vinegar

Toasted sesame oil

Sugar

Butter

Ground cinnamon

serves 4

step **1** make the **asian tofu salad**

step **2** heat the **miso soup**

step **3** make the **broiled bananas with chocolate sorbet**

step **4** **serve**

**heads**up  Most supermarkets sell 4 kinds of tofu: extra-firm, firm, soft, and silken. We use firm here because it slices cleanly and holds together when tossed. If you buy water-packed tofu and don't use it all at once, refrigerate any remaining tofu submerged in water, changing the water daily, for up to 1 week. You may freeze firm and extra-firm tofu for 1 month; freezing makes the tofu even firmer.

*"Tofu, like pasta, needs to be dressed well. You can do wonders with tofu if you keep your pantry well stocked."*

—minutemeals' Chef Wendy

## step 1
### make the **asian tofu salad**

- 2 teaspoons orange marmalade
- 1/2 teaspoon ground ginger
- 1 tablespoon lite soy sauce
- 1 tablespoon rice vinegar
- 1 teaspoon toasted sesame oil
- 1 cup snow peas
- 3 scallions
- 8 ounces firm tofu
- 1 cup matchstick-cut carrots
- 1 bag (5 ounces) prewashed baby spinach, for serving

**1.** In a medium bowl, stir together the marmalade and ginger. Add the soy sauce, vinegar, and sesame oil.

**2.** Coarsely chop the snow peas into 1-inch pieces. Trim and thinly slice the scallions. Cut the tofu into 1-inch cubes.

**3.** Add the snow peas, scallions, tofu, and carrots to the dressing. Toss to coat.

## step 2
### heat the **miso soup**

- 4 packets (41/2 ounces each) white miso soup mix
- 1 quart water

Make the miso soup according to package directions, in 4 individual mugs or bowls.

## step 3
### make the **broiled bananas with chocolate sorbet**

- 1 tablespoon plus 11/2 teaspoons sugar
- 11/2 teaspoons butter, softened
- 1/8 teaspoon ground cinnamon
- 4 ripe bananas
- 2 cups chocolate sorbet, for serving

**1.** Place a cake rack on a jelly-roll pan. In a small bowl, use a fork to blend the sugar, butter, and cinnamon.

**2.** Cut the bananas lengthwise. Spread the butter mixture on the cut side of the bananas, dividing evenly.

**3.** Place the bananas cut-side up on the rack. Preheat the broiler while you serve and eat dinner.

## step 4
### serve

**1.** Divide the baby spinach among 4 large salad plates. Top with the tofu salad, dividing evenly. Serve the salads with the mugs or bowls of miso soup and 6 mini rice cakes per serving.

**2.** When ready for dessert, broil the bananas 4 inches from the heat for 4 minutes, until browned. Place 2 banana halves on each of 4 dessert plates, top each with 1/2 cup chocolate sorbet, and serve.

---

**Asian Tofu Salad**
Single serving is 1/4 of the total menu
CALORIES 452; PROTEIN 15g; CARBS 85g;
TOTAL FAT 7g; SAT FAT 2g; CHOLESTEROL 4mg;
SODIUM 1196mg; FIBER 9g

*15% of calories from fat*

# cool chicken and tortilla soup
## beans and corn relish salad
## sliced oranges with grated chocolate

### shopping list

Corn tortillas (6-inch diameter)

Low-sodium mixed vegetable juice

Sliced roasted chicken breast (Perdue Short Cuts)

Fat-free sour cream

Canned black beans

Canned chickpeas

Jarred corn relish

Lemons (for juice)

Bar of bitter or semisweet chocolate

### from the salad bar

Red onion slices

Cucumber slices

Chopped scallions

Peeled orange sections

### from your pantry

Vegetable cooking spray

Ancho chile powder, or chili powder and cayenne pepper

Ground cumin

Red wine vinegar

Freshly ground black pepper

Sugar

Ground cinnamon

Grand Marnier (optional)

serves 4

## **before**youstart

Chill the vegetable juice. Preheat the oven to 400°F to toast the tortillas.

| step | 1 | make the **cool chicken and tortilla soup** |
| step | 2 | prepare the **beans and corn relish salad** |
| step | 3 | make the **sliced oranges with grated chocolate** |
| step | 4 | **serve** |

## headsup
The little bit of chocolate in dessert makes one tablespoon of chopped chocolate per serving, just enough to give it real panache. Buy a high-quality, flat bar of chocolate (like Lindt), and use a sharp knife to shave thin pieces from the corners, not the long sides, of the bar. The result will be closer to grated chocolate than chopped, without the bother of using a box grater.

*"When it's hot, this is a lovely meal to come home to, whether you make it fresh or a day ahead."*

—minutemeals' Chef Lisa

## step 1

### make the **cool chicken and tortilla soup**

**for the tortillas**

2 corn tortillas (6-inch diameter)

**for the soup**

3/4 cup red onion slices

Vegetable cooking spray

1 tablespoon plus 1/4 teaspoon ancho chile powder, or
1 tablespoon chili powder plus 1/4 teaspoon cayenne pepper

1/2 teaspoon ground cumin

1 bottle (46 ounces) low-sodium mixed vegetable juice, chilled

3 tablespoons red wine vinegar

1 package (5 ounces) sliced roasted chicken breast, cut into bite-sized pieces

4 ice cubes

**for the garnish**

Cucumber slices

Chopped scallions

Fat-free sour cream

1. Preheat the oven to 400°F. Chill the vegetable juice.

2. Halve the tortillas and cut into 1/4-inch-thick strips. Spread them on a baking sheet, preferably one with a nonstick coating. Bake until crisp, 10 to 12 minutes. Remove from the oven and let cool.

3. Chop the onion slices. Coat a medium nonstick skillet with cooking spray, add the onion, cover, and cook over low heat until tender, about 5 minutes, adding a little

water if the onion sticks. Stir in the ancho chile powder and cumin and cook, stirring, 1 minute longer.

4. Transfer the cooked onion to a large bowl and stir in the vegetable juice, vinegar, chicken, and ice cubes. Chill until ready to serve.

5. Dice the chicken into bite-sized pieces. Place the cucumber slices, chopped scallions, and sour cream in separate bowls and bring them to the table.

## step 2

### prepare the **beans and corn relish salad**

1 can (15 ounces) black beans, drained and rinsed

1 can (15 ounces) chickpeas, drained and rinsed

1 jar (13 ounces) corn relish

1/4 cup lemon juice (2 lemons)

Freshly ground black pepper to taste

Drain and rinse the black beans and the chickpeas. In a serving bowl, stir together the beans, corn relish, and lemon juice. Season with pepper. Place the salad on the table with 4 salad plates.

## step 3

### make the **sliced oranges with grated chocolate**

24 ounces orange sections

1 tablespoon sugar

Large pinch ground cinnamon

1 tablespoon Grand Marnier (optional)

1 1/2 ounces semi-sweet chocolate, finely chopped

1. Place the orange sections in a medium bowl. In a small bowl, stir together the sugar and cinnamon.

2. Gently stir the cinnamon-sugar and Grand Marnier, if using, into the oranges. Chill until serving.

3. Coarsely chop the chocolate.

## step 4

### serve

1. Ladle the soup into bowls. Place the cooled tortilla strips in a bowl, and pass them with the garnishes of cucumber, scallions, and sour cream. Serve the soup with the salad.

2. Divide the oranges among 4 dessert dishes and sprinkle each with chocolate, dividing evenly.

---

**Cool Chicken and Tortilla Soup**
Single serving is 1/4 of the total menu
CALORIES 583; PROTEIN 22g; CARBS 105g;
TOTAL FAT 9g; SAT FAT 3g; CHOLESTEROL 15mg;
SODIUM 590mg; FIBER 18g
*14% calories from fat*

# hot and sour soup with chicken and tofu

sticky rice

carrot and cilantro salad

almond baked apricots

## menu gameplan

---

## shopping list

Short- or medium-grain rice

Canned juice-packed apricot halves

Ready-to-use almond filling

Shiitake mushrooms (presliced from the produce department, if available)

Canned sliced bamboo shoots

Chinese chili and garlic paste

Skinless boneless chicken breasts cut for stir-fry

Soft or silken tofu

Chopped scallions (from the salad bar)

Fresh gingerroot

Fresh cilantro sprigs

Grated carrots (from the salad bar or produce department)

## from your pantry

Salt

Fat-free reduced-sodium chicken broth

Rice vinegar

Lite soy sauce

Cornstarch

Brown sugar

Louisiana-style hot sauce

---

serves 4

## beforeyoustart

Bring a medium saucepan of water to a boil, covered. Preheat the oven to 400°F.

step 1   cook the **sticky rice**

step 2   bake the **almond baked apricots**

step 3   cook the **hot and sour soup with chicken and tofu**

step 4   make the **carrot and cilantro salad**

step 5   **serve**

## luckyforyou

Most rice recipes call for measuring the cooking water and paying careful attention to the timing. We cook the short-grain rice here just like pasta. Our method is quicker and easier, and the rice is perfect—in this case, slightly sticky.

*"Here's a recipe that removes the mystery from a Chinese-American classic. And quite a bit of sodium, too."*

—minutemeals' Chef Lisa

## step 1
### cook the **sticky rice**

1 cup short- or medium-grain rice

Salt

Bring a medium saucepan of water to a boil, covered, over high heat. Stir in the rice and generous pinch of salt. Reduce the heat to medium and simmer, uncovered, stirring occasionally, for about 15 minutes, until rice is tender. Drain and return to the saucepan. Toss with a fork over very low heat for 45 seconds to dry out. Cover the saucepan and place on the table.

## step 2
### bake the **almond baked apricots**

1 can (15 ounces) juice-packed apricots, drained, about 2 tablespoons of juice reserved

2 1/2 teaspoons ready-to-use almond filling

1. Preheat the oven to 400°F. Lay apricots cut-sides up in an 8- × 8-inch-square baking dish. Place 1/4 teaspoon almond filling in the hollow of each apricot. Drizzle with the reserved apricot juice.

2. Bake the apricots for 15 minutes. Remove from the oven, and cover with foil to keep warm.

## step 3
### cook the **hot and sour soup with chicken and tofu**

8 ounces shiitake mushrooms, stemmed and sliced

3 cups fat-free reduced-sodium chicken broth

1 cup water

1/2 cup canned sliced bamboo shoots, drained

2 tablespoons rice vinegar

1 tablespoon lite soy sauce

2 teaspoons Chinese chili and garlic paste

8 ounces skinless boneless chicken breasts, cut for stir-fry

4 ounces soft or silken tofu, diced

2 tablespoon cornstarch

1/4 cup chopped scallions

1. Slice the mushroom caps into thin strips.

2. In a large saucepan, stir together the chicken broth, 3/4 cup of the water, the mushrooms, bamboo shoots, rice vinegar, soy sauce, and chili and garlic paste. Cover and bring to a boil. Reduce the heat to medium-low and simmer for 5 minutes.

3. Add the chicken, cover, and simmer 5 minutes, until the chicken is cooked through. Meanwhile, dice the tofu.

4. In a cup, stir together the cornstarch and the remaining water. Stir the mixture into the soup and simmer, stirring often, for 2 minutes. Stir in the tofu and the scallions, cover, and remove from the heat.

## step 4
### make the **carrot and cilantro salad**

3 tablespoons rice or white wine vinegar

1 tablespoon brown sugar

2 teaspoons mild Louisiana-style hot sauce

1/4 teaspoon grated fresh ginger

2 tablespoons coarsely chopped cilantro sprigs

10 ounces grated carrots

1. In a medium bowl, stir together the rice or white wine vinegar, brown sugar, hot sauce, and ginger; whisk until blended.

2. Chop enough cilantro to measure 2 tablespoons. Add the cilantro and grated carrots to the dressing and toss to coat well. Place the bowl on the table with 4 salad plates.

## step 5
### serve

1. Ladle the soup into bowls. Scoop 1/2 cup of sticky rice into 4 small bowls and let diners add it to their soup as they eat. Serve the salad.

2. When ready for dessert, divide the apricots among 4 dessert plates.

---

**Hot and Sour Soup with Chicken and Tofu**
Single serving is 1/4 of the total menu

CALORIES 631; PROTEIN 26g; CARBS 120g; TOTAL FAT 4g; SAT FAT 1g; CHOLESTEROL 31mg; SODIUM 772mg; FIBER 6g

*6% of calories from fat*

# curried chicken noodle soup

### carrot salad with lime
### mango sorbet with pineapple sauce

serves 4

step **1** assemble the **mango sorbet with pineapple sauce**

step **2** assemble the **carrot salad with lime**

step **3** cook the **curried chicken noodle soup**

step **4** serve

## shopping list

Mango sorbet

Scallion

Lime (for juice)

Grape or cherry tomatoes

Frozen broccoli stir-fry mix

Thai curry paste

Chicken breast tenders

Fine egg noodles

Lite coconut milk

Fresh cilantro

### from the salad bar

Cubed fresh pineapple
(or from the produce
department), or juice-
packed canned

Cucumber slices

Shredded carrot (or from the
produce department)

## from your pantry

Sugar

Orange juice

Cayenne pepper

Honey

Salt

Fat-free reduced-sodium
chicken broth

Curry powder

 Using lite coconut milk drastically reduces the calories and saturated fat that would pack this soup if we used regular coconut milk. Lite coconut milk contains only about 40 calories and 2 grams of saturated fat per 1/4-cup serving; regular coconut milk contains a whopping 110 calories and over 10 grams of saturated fat.

*"The chicken soup is East-meets-West comfort food—even more comforting once you see how healthy it is."*

—minutemeals' Chef Sarah

## step 1

### assemble the **mango sorbet with pineapple sauce**

1 cup cubed fresh pineapple, or juice-packed canned, drained

1 tablespoon sugar

1 tablespoon orange juice

Pinch cayenne pepper

1 pint mango sorbet, for serving

1. Coarsely chop the pineapple. Combine the pineapple, sugar, orange juice, and cayenne pepper in a microwave-safe bowl.

2. Microwave the pineapple on High until heated through, 1 to 2 minutes.

## step 2

### assemble the **carrot salad with lime**

1/2 cup cucumber slices

1 scallion

2 tablespoons lime juice (1 lime)

1 tablespoon honey

1/8 teaspoon salt

1/2 cup grape or cherry tomatoes

2 cups shredded carrot

1. Dice the cucumber and slice the scallion. Squeeze 2 tablespoons of juice from the lime.

2. In a medium bowl, mix the lime juice, honey, and salt. Add the cucumber slices, scallion, tomatoes, and carrot; toss to combine. Place the salad on the table with 4 salad plates.

## step 3

### cook the **curried chicken noodle soup**

2 cans (14 ounces each) fat-free reduced-sodium chicken broth

1/2 of a 1-pound bag frozen broccoli stir-fry mix

2–3 teaspoons Thai curry paste

1/2 teaspoon curry powder

1/4 teaspoon salt

1/2 pound chicken breast tenders, cut into 3/4-inch chunks

2 cups fine egg noodles

1/2 cup lite coconut milk

1/2 cup cilantro leaves

1. Bring the broth to a boil in a large pot, covered, over high heat. Stir in the broccoli stir-fry mix, curry paste, curry powder, and salt. Return to a boil, cover, reduce the heat and simmer 5 minutes.

2. While the soup simmers, cut the chicken tenders into 3/4-inch chunks. Stir the chicken and egg noodles into the broth. Cover and simmer 3 to 4 minutes, or until the chicken is cooked through and the noodles are tender.

3. Stir in the coconut milk. Remove the pot from the heat and tear or snip the cilantro leaves into pieces with scissors, adding it to the soup.

## step 4

### serve

1. Ladle the soup into 4 broad, shallow bowls and serve with the salad.

2. When ready for dessert, let the sorbet soften slightly before scooping it into 4 dessert dishes. Spoon the pineapple sauce over and serve.

---

**Curried Chicken Noodle Soup**
Single serving is 1/4 of the total menu
CALORIES 381; PROTEIN 17g; CARBS 68g;
TOTAL FAT 5g; SAT FAT 2g; CHOLESTEROL 47mg;
SODIUM 884mg; FIBER 6g

*12% of calories from fat*

# chicken ravioli and escarole soup
## tomato bruschetta
## grapefruit sorbet

## menu
## gameplan

### shopping list

Escarole

Packaged fresh small chicken-filled ravioli

Whole-wheat Italian bread

Plum tomatoes

Shredded Parmesan cheese

Grapefruit sorbet (2 cups)

### from your pantry

Fat-free reduced-sodium chicken broth

Garlic

Fennel seeds

Dried basil

Red pepper flakes

Balsamic vinegar

Freshly ground black pepper

serves 4

### **before**youstart

Preheat the broiler to toast the bread for the bruschetta.

step **1** cook the **chicken ravioli and escarole soup**

step **2** prepare the **tomato bruschetta**

step **3** serve

**headsup** To make quick work of shredding the escarole, try this Chef's technique: On a chopping board, layer 3 or 4 leaves, aligning the ribs. Split the leaves lengthwise through the ribs, using a very sharp knife, then cut crosswise into narrow ribbons. You need only about half the head of escarole here; refrigerate the other half and use it the next day in salad, alone, or tossed with other greens.

*"I travel with an eye out for meals I can re-create at home. This menu is Italy, quick and healthy."*

—minutemeals' Chef Ruth

### step 1

## cook the **chicken ravioli and escarole soup**

- 2 cans (14 1/2 ounces each) fat-free reduced-sodium chicken broth
- 1 3/4 cups (1 empty broth can) water
- 2 cloves garlic
- 1/4 teaspoon dried basil
- 1/2 teaspoon fennel seeds
- 1/2 head (approximately) fresh escarole
- 1 package (9 ounces) fresh small chicken-filled ravioli
- 1/8 teaspoon crushed red pepper flakes

**1.** Place the chicken broth and water in a large heavy saucepan. Mince the garlic and add to the broth with the dried basil and the fennel seeds. Cover and bring to a boil over high heat.

**2.** Finely shred enough escarole to measure 2 cups, firmly packed.

**3.** Add the ravioli and the escarole to the boiling broth. Cover, reduce the heat to medium, and simmer about 8 minutes, stirring often, until the pasta is tender. Season to taste with crushed red pepper flakes. Cover and keep warm until serving time.

### step 2

## prepare the **tomato bruschetta**

- 8 thin slices (about 1/2 ounce each) whole wheat Italian bread
- 4 plum tomatoes, chopped
- 1 tablespoon balsamic vinegar
- Freshly ground pepper to taste
- 8 teaspoons (2 tablespoons plus 2 teaspoons) shredded Parmesan cheese

**1.** Preheat the broiler. Place the Italian bread slices on a jelly-roll pan. Broil the bread 6 inches from the heat for 3 to 5 minutes, turning once, until both sides are lightly toasted.

**2.** Roughly chop the plum tomatoes. Add the balsamic vinegar and pepper and mix gently but well.

**3.** Transfer the toasts to a serving plate. Mound the tomato mixture on the toasts, dividing evenly. Sprinkle 1 teaspoon of cheese on top of each toast. Set the platter on the table with bread and butter plates.

### step 3

## serve

**1.** Ladle the soup into 4 broad soup bowls, dividing evenly. Pass the bruschetta, allowing 2 per diner.

**2.** When ready for dessert, scoop 1/2 cup of grapefruit sorbet into 4 dessert dishes and serve.

---

**Chicken Ravioli and Escarole Soup**
Single serving is 1/4 of the total menu
CALORIES 360; PROTEIN 14g; CARBS 61g; TOTAL FAT 8g; SAT FAT 4g; CHOLESTEROL 38mg; SODIUM 1038mg; FIBER 6g
*20% of calories from fat*

# hungarian goulash soup
## cucumber salad with dill
## warm rye toasts
## crisp apples with honey

menu
**game**plan

### shopping list

Beef sirloin tips

Presliced portobello mushrooms (from the produce department)

Canned seasoned diced tomatoes

Fat-free sour cream

Scallion

Fresh dill

Marble rye bread

Crisp, tart apples (4)

### from the salad bar

Green pepper slices

Red onion slices

Cucumber slices

### from your pantry

Canola oil

Paprika

Salt and pepper

Fat-free reduced-sodium beef broth

Red wine vinegar

Sugar

Caraway seeds

Onion powder

Olive oil cooking spray

Honey

serves 4

### **before**youstart

Preheat the oven to 450°F to toast the rye bread. Rinse the apples and chill.

step **1** cook the **hungarian goulash soup**

step **2** assemble the **cucumber salad with dill**

step **3** prepare the **warm rye toasts**

step **4** **serve**

## **heads**up
You don't want to overcook the flavorful beef sirloin tips in this dish. Unlike tougher cuts of stew beef, it won't get more tender the longer it cooks. Taste as you cook to check for doneness. You can use diced tomatoes flavored with either roasted garlic or with green pepper, celery, and onions.

*"Hearty food doesn't have to be unhealthy. This meal is warm and filling, and good for you, too."*

—minutemeals' Chef Sarah

## step 1

### cook the **hungarian goulash soup**

3/4 pound beef sirloin tips

1 package (6 ounces) presliced portobello mushrooms

1 cup green pepper slices

1/2 cup red onion slices

2 teaspoons canola oil

2 teaspoons paprika

Pepper to taste

1 can (14 1/2 ounces) seasoned diced tomatoes

1 can (14 ounces) fat-free reduced-sodium beef broth

1/4 cup fat-free sour cream, for serving

**1.** Cut the beef into bite-sized pieces. Coarsely chop the mushrooms, green pepper, and onion slices.

**2.** Heat the oil in a large pot over medium-high heat for 1 minute. Add the beef, green pepper, and onion to the pot. Cook, stirring often, for 3 minutes, or until the beef is lightly browned.

**3.** Stir in the mushrooms and paprika. Season with pepper. Cook, stirring, for 2 minutes.

**4.** Add the diced tomatoes and beef broth, cover, and bring to a boil. Reduce the heat to medium-low and simmer, uncovered, 10 minutes, or until the beef is tender.

## step 2

### assemble the **cucumber salad with dill**

1 scallion, sliced

2 tablespoons snipped fresh dill

4 cups cucumber slices

1/4 cup red wine vinegar

2 tablespoons sugar

1/8 teaspoon salt

Pepper to taste

**1.** Slice the scallion. Chop enough dill to measure 2 tablespoons.

**2.** In a salad bowl, place the scallion, dill, cucumber slices, vinegar, and sugar. Season with salt and pepper and toss to mix.

## step 3

### prepare the **warm rye toasts**

4 slices marble rye bread

1/2 teaspoon caraway seeds

1/4 teaspoon onion powder

Olive oil cooking spray

**1.** Preheat the oven to 450°F. Place the bread slices on a cookie sheet. Sprinkle with the caraway seeds and onion powder. Spray with the olive oil spray.

**2.** Bake for 5 minutes, or until toasted.

## step 4

### serve

**1.** Ladle the soup into 4 soup bowls. Place the sour cream in a small bowl and pass as a garnish for the soup.

**2.** Place 4 salad plates on the table. Cut the rye toasts in half and place on a serving plate. Place the salad and toasts on the table.

**3.** When ready for dessert, place 1 apple on each of 4 dessert plates with a small, sharp knife. Pour 1/4 cup honey in a small bowl, and let diners slice and dip their apples into the honey.

Hungarian Goulash Soup
Single serving is 1/4 of the total menu

CALORIES 454; PROTEIN 24g; CARBS 75g; TOTAL FAT 9g; SAT FAT 2g; CHOLESTEROL 45mg; SODIUM 1075mg; FIBER 9g

*17% of calories from fat*

# mexican meatball soup

## green salad with warm corn vinaigrette

## ambrosial angel food cake

menu
**game**plan

serves 4

step **1** cook the **mexican meatball soup**

step **2** assemble the **ambrosial angel food cake**

step **3** make the **green salad with warm corn vinaigrette**

step **4** **serve**

### shopping list

Canned diced tomatoes with green chiles

Lean ground beef

Reduced-fat shredded Monterey jack cheese

Fresh fettuccine

Zucchini

Fresh cilantro

Canned mandarin orange sections in pear juice or light syrup

Banana

Fresh pineapple chunks (from the salad bar)

Angel food cake

Sweetened shredded coconut

Red onion slices (from the salad bar)

Frozen corn kernels

Prewashed spring greens mix

### from your pantry

Fat-free reduced-sodium chicken broth

Minced garlic in oil

Ground cumin

Salt

Red wine vinegar

Olive oil

Chili powder

**heads**up If you're not in the mood for Mexican, you can turn this into Italian meatball soup. Simply replace the cumin with Italian seasoning, substitute mozzarella cheese for the Monterey jack, and use diced tomatoes flavored with Italian seasoning instead of green chiles.

*"This soup is especially nice on a cool night—kind of like spaghetti and meatballs, but quicker."*

—minutemeals' Chef Sarah

## step 1

### cook the **mexican meatball soup**

1 can (14 ounces) fat-free reduced-sodium chicken broth

1³/₄ cups (1 empty broth can) water

1 can (10 ounces) diced tomatoes with green chiles

1¹/₂ teaspoons minced garlic in oil

1 teaspoon ground cumin

¹/₂ pound lean ground beef

¹/₂ cup reduced-fat shredded Monterey jack cheese

¹/₂ of a 9-ounce package fresh fettuccine

1 large zucchini

2 tablespoons chopped fresh cilantro, for serving

1. In a large saucepan or Dutch oven, bring the chicken broth, water, tomatoes with chiles, 1 teaspoon of the garlic, and the cumin to a boil, covered, over high heat. Reduce the heat and simmer 5 for minutes.

2. Meanwhile, in a medium bowl, combine the remaining ¹/₂ teaspoon garlic, the ground beef, Monterey jack cheese, and salt until well mixed. Shape the meat mixture into rough 1-inch meatballs. (The meat won't stick to your hands if you wet them slightly with cool water.) Drop the meatballs into the tomato mixture, cover, and simmer 4 minutes.

3. Meanwhile, with kitchen scissors, cut the fettuccine into 1¹/₂-inch lengths. Dice the zucchini. Add the fettuccine and zucchini to the broth. Return to a boil; reduce the heat, cover, and simmer 2 to 3 minutes longer, or until the pasta is cooked. Chop enough cilantro to measure 2 tablespoons

## step 2

### assemble the **ambrosial angel food cake**

1 can (11 ounces) mandarin oranges in pear juice or light syrup

1 small banana, sliced

1 cup fresh pineapple chunks

4 slices (1 ounce each) angel food cake

2 tablespoons sweetened shredded coconut

1. Drain the mandarin oranges, reserving 2 tablespoons of the juice or syrup. Slice the banana.

2. Combine the mandarin oranges and the reserved juice, banana, and pineapple chunks in a medium bowl. Arrange the cake slices on 4 dessert plates.

## step 3

### make the **green salad with warm corn vinaigrette**

2 red onion slices, chopped

1 cup frozen corn kernels

2 tablespoons red wine vinegar

2 teaspoons olive oil

³/₄ teaspoon chili powder

¹/₄ teaspoon salt

1 bag (5 ounces) prewashed spring greens

1. Chop the red onion slices. Combine the red onion, corn, vinegar, olive oil, chili powder, and salt in a large microwave-safe bowl. Cover with vented plastic wrap and microwave on High, 2 minutes, or until heated through.

2. Add the spring greens to the vinaigrette and toss. Place the salad on the table with 4 salad plates.

## step 4

### serve

1. Ladle the soup into 4 bowls and sprinkle some of the cilantro over each. Serve with the salad.

2. When ready for dessert, spoon the fruit over the cake slices and sprinkle each serving with coconut.

**Mexican Meatball Soup**
Single serving is ¹/₄ of the total menu
CALORIES 438; PROTEIN 23g; CARBS 68g;
TOTAL FAT 10g; SAT FAT 4g; CHOLESTEROL 56mg;
SODIUM 1016mg; FIBER 8g
*21% of calories from fat*

# thai corn and tofu soup
## cucumber salad
## mango sorbet

menu
**game**plan

serves 4

| step | 1 | make the **thai corn and tofu soup** |
| --- | --- | --- |
| step | 2 | make the **cucumber salad** |
| step | 3 | **serve** |

## shopping list
Shallot

Enriched firm tofu

Canned corn with red and green peppers

Lite coconut milk

Fresh cilantro

Lime (for juice)

English cucumber

Fresh dill

Lemon (for zest)

Reduced-fat sour cream

Mango sorbet

## from your pantry
Olive oil cooking spray

Ground cayenne pepper

Vegetable broth

Salt

Freshly ground black pepper

## headsup
Cilantro is generally sold in large bunches. To store bunches with roots attached, stand the roots in water and cover the container with a plastic bag. Refrigerate for up to 1 week, changing the water every 2 days. If the roots have been trimmed, wrap the stems in damp paper towels and enclose the whole bunch in plastic wrap; refrigerate for 3 days. The roots, which are edible, may be frozen.

*"This soup contains no dairy, and no meat, yet it's creamy and filling. The corn gives it a nice crunch."*

—minutemeals' Chef Wendy

## step 1

### make the **thai corn and tofu soup**

1 medium shallot

Olive oil cooking spray

1 pound enriched firm tofu

1 can (11 ounces) corn with red and green peppers

1/2 teaspoon ground cayenne pepper

1 cup lite coconut milk

1 can (14 1/2 ounces) vegetable broth

2 tablespoons chopped fresh cilantro

1 tablespoon lime juice

**1.** Finely chop the shallot. Coat a large heavy saucepan with olive oil spray and place over medium-high heat. Add the shallot and cook 3 minutes, stirring occasionally, or until tender.

**2.** Coarsely chop the tofu into rough 1-inch pieces. Add the tofu to the saucepan and cook, stirring occasionally, about 4 minutes or until browned. Stir in the corn and cayenne pepper.

**3.** Add the coconut milk and vegetable broth. Increase the heat and bring to a boil. Reduce to a simmer and cook 5 minutes.

**4.** Chop enough cilantro to measure 2 tablespoons. Remove the soup from the heat. Squeeze 1 tablespoon of juice from the lime. Add the cilantro and lime juice to the soup.

## step 2

### make the **cucumber salad**

1 English cucumber

2 tablespoons chopped fresh dill

1 tablespoon lemon zest

1/4 cup reduced-fat sour cream

Salt and freshly ground black pepper to taste

**1.** Cut the cucumber into thin discs. Chop enough dill to measure 2 tablespoons. Grate 1 teaspoon of zest from the lemon.

**2.** In a medium bowl mix the sour cream, dill, and lemon zest. Add the cucumber and toss to coat. Season with salt and pepper.

## step 3

### serve

**1.** Ladle the soup into 4 bowls and bring to the table with the salad.

**2.** When ready for dessert, scoop 1/2 cup of the sorbet into each of 4 bowls.

---

**Thai Corn and Tofu Soup**
Single serving is 1/4 of the total menu
CALORIES 291; PROTEIN 11g; CARBS 46g;
TOTAL FAT 9g; SAT FAT 4g; CHOLESTEROL 8mg;
SODIUM 893mg; FIBER 3g
*26% of calories from fat*

# corn, tomato, and black bean chowder
## boston lettuce salad
## sourdough rolls
## lemon ice with blueberries

**menu**
**game**plan

## shopping list

Fresh blueberries

Lemon ice

Low-sodium diced tomatoes

Frozen corn kernels

Canned black beans

Fresh basil

Sourdough rolls

Boston lettuce

Watercress

Belgian endive

Matchstick-cut carrots (from the produce department)

Reduced-fat Dijon salad dressing

## from your pantry

Sugar

Ground cinnamon

Garlic

Fat-free reduced-sodium chicken broth

Dried marjoram

Dried oregano

Freshly ground black pepper

serves 4

## **before**youstart

Preheat the toaster oven to warm the rolls.

step **1** prepare the **lemon ice with blueberries**

step **2** cook the **corn, tomato, and black bean chowder**

step **3** warm the **sourdough rolls**

step **4** make the **boston lettuce salad**

step **5** **serve**

## heads up
We add the dried herbs when we start the soup because they need heat and moisture to bring out their flavor. On the other hand, fresh basil is at its most flavorful and aromatic when raw or briefly warmed, so we add it at the end of the cooking process.

*"You don't need complicated techniques or fancy ingredients to give a meal real pizzazz. Herbs and seasonings do the trick."*

—minutemeals' Chef Hillary

## step 1

### prepare the **lemon ice with blueberries**

2 cups fresh blueberries, rinsed and picked over

1 tablespoon sugar

Pinch ground cinnamon

4 individual servings of lemon ice, for serving

Rinse the blueberries and discard any that are green or soft. In a medium bowl, stir together the blueberries, sugar, and cinnamon.

## step 2

### cook the **corn, tomato, and black bean chowder**

2 garlic cloves, chopped

1 can (14$\frac{1}{2}$ ounces) fat-free reduced-sodium chicken broth

1 can (14$\frac{1}{2}$ ounces) low-sodium diced tomatoes

1 package (10 ounces) frozen corn kernels

$\frac{1}{2}$ teaspoon dried marjoram

$\frac{1}{4}$ teaspoon dried oregano

Freshly ground black pepper to taste

1 can (15 ounces) black beans

$\frac{1}{2}$ cup chopped fresh basil

1. Chop the garlic. In a large, heavy saucepan, place the garlic, chicken broth, tomatoes, corn, marjoram, oregano, and pepper. Stir until well blended. Cover and bring to a boil over high heat. Reduce the heat to low and simmer for 5 to 7 minutes.

2. While the soup simmers, drain and rinse the black beans. Stir the beans into the soup and simmer 5 minutes longer. Chop enough basil to measure $\frac{1}{2}$ cup. Remove the soup from the heat and stir in the basil. Cover to keep warm.

## step 3

### warm the **sourdough rolls**

4 sourdough rolls

Heat the rolls in a toaster oven according to the directions on the package. Wrap in a napkin to keep warm, and place in a basket.

## step 4

### make the **boston lettuce salad**

1 large head Boston lettuce

1 bunch watercress

1 large Belgian endive

$\frac{1}{2}$ cup matchstick-cut carrots

2 tablespoons reduced-fat Dijon salad dressing

Freshly ground black pepper to taste

1. Tear the lettuce leaves into bite-sized pieces and place in the bowl of a salad spinner. Discard the tough stems from the watercress and add the leaves to the lettuce. Cut the endive into very thin slices on an angle and add to the salad greens. Rinse the greens and spin dry.

2. Transfer the dry greens to a salad bowl. Add the carrots, dressing, and pepper. Toss, and place on the table with 4 salad plates.

## step 5

### serve

1. Ladle the soup into large bowls and serve with the salad and warm rolls.

2. When ready for dessert, place the ices in individual dessert dishes or bowls. Spoon about $\frac{1}{2}$ cup of the blueberries over each, and serve.

**Corn, Tomato, and Black Bean Chowder**
Single serving is $\frac{1}{4}$ of the total menu
CALORIES 427; PROTEIN 14g; CARBS 89g; TOTAL FAT 4g; SAT FAT 1g; CHOLESTEROL 1mg; SODIUM 1046mg; FIBER 12g

*8% of calories from fat*

minute

quick

# poultry

meals
& healthy

# greek chicken
## with orzo

### tomatoes with creamy dressing

### figs in port and honey

## menu gameplan

### shopping list

Frozen chopped onion

Zucchini

Orzo

Chicken tenders

Prewashed baby spinach leaves

Crumbled feta cheese

Vine-ripe tomatoes

Red onion

Low-fat Ranch dressing

Small fresh figs

### from your pantry

Fat-free reduced-sodium chicken broth

Dried oregano

Freshly ground black pepper

Port wine

Sugar

Honey

serves 4

step **1** cook the **greek chicken with orzo**

step **2** make the **tomatoes with creamy dressing**

step **3** prepare the **figs in port and honey**

step **4** **serve**

**heads**up Orzo is rice-shaped pasta and is usually cooked like pasta, in a large amount of boiling water. We opted instead to simmer it in a small amount of broth so that the starch from the pasta "grains" creates a creamy sauce, much like Arborio rice does in risotto. But unlike risotto, our dish doesn't require 25 minutes of nonstop stirring.

*"You can skip the salad here and still have a balanced meal: pasta, chicken, and green vegetables, in one bowl."*
—minutemeals' Chef Paul

## cook the **greek chicken with orzo**

1 can (14 1/2 ounces) fat-free, reduced-sodium chicken broth

1 1/2 cups water

1 1/2 cups frozen chopped onion

2 medium zucchini

2 cups orzo (12 ounces)

12 ounces chicken tenders

1 1/2 teaspoons dried oregano

1 package (5 ounces) pre-washed baby spinach leaves

Pepper to taste

1/2 cup crumbled feta cheese

**1.** Put the broth, water, and onion in a Dutch oven or large saucepan. Cover and bring to a boil over medium-high heat. Quarter the zucchini lengthwise and slice crosswise. Stir the orzo and zucchini into the broth. Return to a boil, reduce the heat, cover, and simmer for 4 minutes, stirring occasionally.

**2.** Stir in the chicken tenders and oregano. Return to a boil. Cover and cook 6 minutes longer, until the chicken is cooked through and the orzo is tender. Stir in the spinach until wilted. Remove from the heat, season with pepper, and sprinkle with the feta. Cover to keep warm.

## step 2

## make the **tomatoes with creamy dressing**

6 medium vine-ripe tomatoes

1 small red onion

4 tablespoons low-fat Ranch dressing

Freshly ground black pepper to taste

Slice the tomatoes. Slice the onion and separate into rings. Arrange the tomato slices and onion rings on 4 salad plates, and drizzle each serving with 1 tablespoon of the dressing. Grind a generous amount of black pepper over each salad.

## step 3

## prepare the **figs in port and honey**

1/2 cup port wine

1 tablespoon sugar

1 tablespoon honey

12 small fresh figs

Combine the port, sugar, and honey in a microwave-safe dish. Microwave on High for 1 minute. Divide the figs among 4 small dessert dishes and spoon some of the warm port mixture over each serving.

## step 4

## serve

**1.** Divide the orzo mixture among 4 shallow pasta bowls, and serve with the tomato and onion salads.

**2.** When ready for dessert, serve the figs with port sauce.

---

**Greek Chicken with Orzo**
Single serving is 1/4 of the total menu
CALORIES 707; PROTEIN 36g; CARBS 113g;
TOTAL FAT 12g; SAT FAT 4g; CHOLESTEROL 68mg;
SODIUM 876mg; FIBER 11g

*15% of calories from fat*

# chicken, fennel, and white bean stew

## lemon-garlic angel hair pasta

## apples with praline dip

### menu gameplan

serves 4

### beforeyoustart

Bring the water to a boil in a large saucepan, covered, over high heat, to cook the angel hair pasta.

**step 1** cook the **chicken, fennel, and white bean stew**

**step 2** while the chicken cooks, make the **lemon-garlic angel hair pasta**

**step 3** prepare the **apples with praline dip**

**step 4** serve

---

### shopping list

Frozen chopped onion

Fennel bulb

Canned white beans

Chicken tenders

Angel hair pasta

Roasted garlic in purée

Lemon juice

Reduced-fat sour cream

Tart apples

### from your pantry

Orange juice

Fat-free reduced-sodium chicken broth

Fennel seeds

Balsamic vinegar

Salt

Freshly ground black pepper

Olive oil

Brown sugar

Ground cinnamon

luckyforyou Canned beans are a convenient (and cheap) source of low-fat protein as well as fiber. If you are trying to reduce the amount of animal protein you use without radically changing your family's diet, a dish like this one, which combines beans with a familiar protein, is the way to go.

*"Orange and fennel work so well together. The combination gives this homey dish a bit of sophistication."*

—minutemeals' Chef Marge

## step 1

### cook the **chicken, fennel, and white bean stew**

1/2 cup orange juice

1/2 cup fat-free reduced-sodium chicken broth

3/4 cup frozen chopped onions

1 fennel bulb

1 teaspoon fennel seeds

1 can (15 ounces) small white beans, drained and rinsed

12 ounces chicken tenders

2 tablespoons balsamic vinegar

1. Heat the orange juice, chicken broth, and frozen onions in a large skillet over medium heat. Cut the fennel bulb in half, cut out the core, and slice crosswise into thin strips. Add the fennel to the skillet, bring to a boil, cover, and cook for 4 minutes, or until fennel is tender.

2. Meanwhile, place the fennel seeds in a self-sealing plastic bag and crush lightly with a rolling pin or small skillet. Add to the skillet.

3. Drain and rinse the beans. Stir the chicken tenders into the skillet, pressing to cover them with the broth and fennel. Spread the beans on top. Bring to a simmer, cover, and cook for 7 minutes or until the chicken is cooked through. Stir in the balsamic vinegar and season with salt and pepper. Remove from the heat.

## step 2

### make the **lemon-garlic angel hair pasta**

3 quarts water

Salt

8 ounces angel hair pasta

2 teaspoons olive oil

2 teaspoons roasted garlic in purée

2 teaspoons lemon juice

Freshly ground black pepper to taste

1. Bring the water to a boil in a large saucepan, covered, over high heat. Salt lightly. Add the pasta and cook according to package directions, or until *al dente*. Drain well and return to the pasta-cooking pot.

2. Add the olive oil, garlic, and lemon juice, and season with ground black pepper.

## step 3

### prepare the **apples with praline dip**

3 tablespoons reduced-fat sour cream

1 1/2 tablespoons packed brown sugar

Generous pinch ground cinnamon

4 tart apples, for serving

Stir together the sour cream, brown sugar, and cinnamon in a small bowl. Refrigerate until ready for dessert.

## step 4

### serve

1. Divide the pasta among 4 dinner plates. Spoon the chicken and fennel mixture over pasta, dividing evenly. Serve.

2. When ready for dessert, halve the apples, core, and cut into wedges. Place the wedges in a bowl. Place the wedges on the table with 4 small dessert dishes. Serve the apples with the praline dip.

---

**Chicken, Fennel, and White Bean Stew**
Single serving is 1/4 of the total menu
CALORIES 486; PROTEIN 29g; CARBS 76g;
TOTAL FAT 8g; SAT FAT 2g; CHOLESTEROL 53mg;
SODIUM 719mg; FIBER 8g

*14% of calories from fat*

# golden chicken nuggets

## boiled new potatoes with garlic and parsley

## mixed green salad

## peaches with raspberry sauce

### shopping list

Chicken tenders

Pre-trimmed and scrubbed new potatoes

Fresh parsley

Grape tomatoes

Prewashed spring or baby greens

Raspberries

Frozen sliced peaches

### from your pantry

Vegetable cooking spray

All-purpose flour

Cornstarch

Eggs

Cornflake crumbs

Garlic

Olive oil

Salt

Low-fat vinaigrette dressing, store-bought

Honey

## menu gameplan

serves 4

### beforeyoustart

Preheat the oven to 375°F to cook the chicken.

step 1    cook the **golden chicken nuggets**

step 2    cook the **boiled new potatoes with garlic and parsley**

step 3    assemble the **mixed green salad**

step 4    prepare the **peaches with raspberry sauce**

step 5    **serve**

## luckyforyou

Chicken tenders require no cutting and come nicely bite-sized. They give you a big jump-start on the preparation here.

*"Wouldn't you rather decide what goes into the chicken nuggets you give your family? I would, which is why I created the recipe."*

—minutemeals' Chef Marge

### step 1
## cook the **golden chicken nuggets**

Vegetable cooking spray

1 pound chicken tenders

2 tablespoons all-purpose flour

2 tablespoons cornstarch

2 large egg whites

3/4 cup cornflakes crumbs

1. Preheat the oven to 375°F. Coat a baking sheet with cooking spray. Cut the chicken tenders in half crosswise.

2. Mix the flour and cornstarch together in a shallow bowl. In another bowl, beat the egg whites together lightly. Spread the cornflakes out on a plate.

3. Working with 1 piece of chicken at a time, dredge the chicken in the flour mixture. Dip it next into the egg whites, then roll in the cornflakes crumbs coating all sides.

4. Place the chicken pieces in 1 layer on the prepared baking sheet. Bake for 10 minutes, or until the pieces are cooked through.

### step 2
## cook the **boiled new potatoes with garlic and parsley**

1 pound pre-trimmed and scrubbed new potatoes

1/4 cup chopped fresh parsley

2 garlic cloves

1 cup grape tomatoes

1 tablespoon olive oil

Salt to taste (optional)

1. Place the potatoes in a medium saucepan, add water to cover, and bring to a boil over high heat. Simmer for 12 to 15 minutes, or until tender when tested with a fork.

2. While the potatoes cook, chop enough parsley to measure 1/4 cup; finely chop the garlic.

3. Drain the potatoes, place in a bowl, and add the grape tomatoes, parsley, garlic, and olive oil. Toss to combine. Sprinkle with salt, if desired, and place the bowl on the table.

### step 3
## assemble the **mixed green salad**

1 bag (5 ounces) prewashed spring or baby greens

2 tablespoons store-bought low-fat vinaigrette dressing

Place the greens in a salad bowl, add the vinaigrette, and toss to coat. Place the bowl on the table.

### step 4
## prepare the **peaches with raspberry sauce**

1 pint fresh raspberries

1 tablespoon honey

2 cups frozen sliced peaches

1. Rinse the raspberries in a colander and shake dry. Place in a food processor or blender. Add the honey and purée. Pour the sauce into a serving bowl.

2. Thaw the sliced peaches in a microwave oven according to the directions on the package.

### step 5
## serve

1. Divide the chicken nuggets among 4 dinner plates and serve immediately with the potatoes and salad.

2. When ready for dessert, divide the peaches among 4 dessert bowls. Serve with the raspberry sauce for spooning over the top.

**Golden Chicken Nuggets**
Single serving is 1/4 of the total menu

CALORIES 441; PROTEIN 32g; CARBS 62g;
TOTAL FAT 8g; SAT FAT 1g; CHOLESTEROL 63mg;
SODIUM 480mg; FIBER 8g

*16% of calories from fat*

# orange adobo chicken

### rice with pinto beans
### spinach salad
### fruit-juice bars

## shopping list

Skinless boneless chicken breasts

Orange slices
(from the salad bar)

Red onion slices
(from the salad bar)

Radishes

Cilantro

Pimento-stuffed green olives

Canned pinto beans

Prewashed baby spinach

Unsalted pumpkin or sunflower seeds

Frozen fruit-juice bars

## from your pantry

Ground cumin

Dried oregano

Salt

Freshly ground black pepper

10-minute boil-in-bag white rice

Olive oil

Paprika

Reduced-fat vinaigrette dressing

serves 4

## **before**youstart

Bring the water to a boil in a medium saucepan, covered, over high heat, to cook the rice.

| step 1 | cook the **orange adobo chicken** |
| step 2 | cook the **rice with pinto beans** |
| step 3 | make the **spinach salad** |
| step 4 | **serve** |

## headsup

There are a number of things you can do to tweak this menu each time you make it—and you will make it again and again. Use hot paprika in the rice to add a smoky-spicy note to the menu or substitute pork chops or turkey cutlets for the chicken. Time permitting, grate 1 teaspoon of orange zest and add it to the chicken spice rub.

*"A trip to the salad bar, not Mexico, inspired the chicken. I saw oranges, onions, and radishes—I had my salsa."*
—minutemeals' Chef Sarah

## step 1

### cook the **orange adobo chicken**

- 1 teaspoon ground cumin
- 1/2 teaspoon dried oregano
- 1/4 teaspoon salt
- 1/4 teaspoon freshly ground black pepper to taste
- 4 skinless boneless chicken breasts (4 to 5 ounces each)
- 2 cups orange slices (about 15 ounces) chopped
- 2 red onion slices, chopped
- 6 radishes, chopped
- 1/2 cup cilantro, chopped
- 1/4 cup small pimento-stuffed green olives, chopped

1. Combine the cumin, oregano, salt, and pepper in a small bowl. Sprinkle the spice mixture over the chicken breasts, pressing so that it adheres to the meat.

2. Heat a nonstick grill pan over medium heat. Place the chicken breasts in the pan and grill 4 to 5 minutes per side, or until cooked through. Transfer the chicken to a plate.

3. While the chicken cooks, dice the oranges and chop the red onion, radishes, cilantro, and olives. Combine the oranges, onion, radishes, cilantro, and olives in a small bowl. Season with additional salt and pepper.

## step 2

### cook the **rice with pinto beans**

- 1 bag (2-cup size) 10-minute boil-in-bag white rice
- 1 teaspoon olive oil
- 1 cup canned pinto beans, rinsed and drained
- 1/2 teaspoon paprika
- 1/4 teaspoon salt

1. Cook the rice according to the package directions.

2. Remove the rice bag from the boiling water and let drain. In the rice-cooking pot, heat the olive oil and add the pinto beans, paprika, and salt. Cook, stirring, for 1 minute. Add the rice, place over low heat, and cook, stirring, for 1 minute, until heated through. Cover and keep warm until serving.

## step 3

### make the **spinach salad**

- 1 bag (5 ounces) prewashed baby spinach
- 2 tablespoons unsalted pumpkin or sunflower seeds
- 2 tablespoons reduced-fat vinaigrette dressing
- Freshly ground black pepper to taste

Place the spinach, pumpkin or sunflower seeds, and vinaigrette dressing in a salad bowl. Season with pepper and toss. Place the salad bowl on the table.

## step 4

### serve

1. Divide the chicken breasts among 4 dinner plates, and pass the orange salsa to spoon over top.

2. Turn the rice in a serving bowl and place on the table.

3. When ready fo dessert, serve 1 fruit-juice bar to each diner.

---

**Orange Adobo Chicken**
Single serving is 1/4 of the total menu
CALORIES 679; PROTEIN 41g; CARBS 94g;
TOTAL FAT 11g; SAT FAT 3g; CHOLESTEROL 63mg;
SODIUM 888mg; FIBER 11g
*22% of calories from fat*

# grilled chicken
## with mexican peanut sauce

steamed snow peas and red peppers

flour tortillas

mango porcupines

## shopping list

Small ripe mangoes

Skinless boneless chicken breasts

Scallion

Chipotle chile en adobo

Canned no-salt-added tomato sauce

Lime

Red pepper slices
(from the salad bar)

Stringed snow or sugar snap peas

Fat-free flour tortillas
(8-inch diameter)

## from your pantry

Honey

Olive oil cooking spray

Salt and pepper

Peanut butter

Chili powder

Ground cinnamon

Instant coffee granules

serves 4

**step 1** prepare the **mango porcupines**

**step 2** cook the **grilled chicken with mexican peanut sauce**

**step 3** while the chicken cooks, steam the **snow peas and red peppers**

**step 4** serve

## headsup

Chipotles are dried, smoked jalapeño chiles, and they are spicy indeed. We recommend removing the seeds and veins before using, since they contain the great majority of the heat-causing compound capsaicin. Be very careful while handling hot chiles; capsaicin can burn and irritate your skin and eyes. Wear gloves while you work, or wash your hands well immediately after handling the chiles.

*"Everything in moderation: Here that thing is peanut butter, just enough to make a really distinctive sauce."*

—minutemeals' Chef Paul

### step 1

#### prepare the **mango porcupines**

> 2 small ripe mangoes
>
> 1 tablespoon honey, for serving

1. Stand a mango on its wide end on a cutting board. Slice down the length of the mango, keeping the knife just off-center and close to the pit. Repeat on the other side. Discard the center pit piece. Repeat with the remaining mango.

2. Score the flesh of the mango halves in a checkerboard pattern, taking care not to cut through the skin. Push up from the skin side so that the cubes separate and jut out. Place a mango half on each of 4 dessert dishes.

### step 2

#### cook the **grilled chicken with mexican peanut sauce**

> Olive oil cooking spray
>
> 4 skinless boneless chicken breasts (4 ounces each)
>
> Salt and pepper to taste
>
> 1 scallion
>
> 1 small chipotle chile en adobo
>
> 1 can (8 ounces) no-salt-added tomato sauce
>
> 1 1/2 tablespoons peanut butter
>
> 1 tablespoon water
>
> 3/4 teaspoon chili powder
>
> 1/2 teaspoon ground cinnamon
>
> 1/2 teaspoon instant coffee granules

1. Spray a grill pan with olive oil cooking spray and heat over medium heat. Season the chicken with salt and pepper. Place the chicken in the pan and grill for 8 to 10 minutes, turning once, until cooked through.

2. While the chicken cooks, prepare the sauce: Trim the scallion and cut it into 1-inch pieces. Seed the chipotle chile. Place the scallion and chile in a blender or mini-processor. Add the tomato sauce, peanut butter, water, chili powder, cinnamon, and coffee granules. Process until smooth. Scrape the sauce into a small saucepan. Bring to a simmer over medium-high heat and simmer 4 minutes, stirring occasionally. Cover to keep warm.

### step 3

#### while the chicken cooks, make the **steamed snow peas and red peppers**

> 1 lime
>
> 1 cup red pepper slices (about 4 ounces)
>
> 1 package (8 ounces) stringed snow or sugar snap peas
>
> Salt and pepper to taste

1. Cut the lime into 8 wedges to serve with both the snow peas and mango.

2. Place the red pepper slices in a microwave-safe dish and cover with a lid or vented plastic wrap. Microwave on High for 2 to 3 minutes.

Stir in the snow or sugar snap peas and microwave on High for 2 minutes longer, until the snow peas are tender and bright green. Season with salt and pepper.

### step 4

#### serve

1. Place 4 tortillas on a small plate. Cover with a paper towel and microwave on for High 40 seconds.

2. Place a piece of chicken on each of 4 dinner plates and spoon some of the sauce over. Spoon a serving of snow peas and red peppers next to the chicken, and place a wedge of lime on the plate. Serve with the warm tortillas.

3. When ready for dessert, drizzle the mango pieces with the honey and serve with the remaining lime wedges.

---

**Grilled Chicken with Mexican Peanut Sauce**
**Single serving is 1/4 of the total menu**
CALORIES 410; PROTEIN 30g; CARBS 61g;
TOTAL FAT 7g; SAT FAT 1g; CHOLESTEROL 63mg;
SODIUM 599mg; FIBER 7g

*14% of calories from fat*

# chicken cutlets
## with pear-applesauce

jasmine rice with shallots

micro-steamed sugar snap peas and carrots

angel food cake with chocolate-espresso sauce

**menu**
**game**plan

### shopping list

Shallot

Jasmine rice

Skinless boneless chicken breast halves

Pears

Unsweetened applesauce

Stringed sugar snap peas

Matchstick-cut carrots (from the produce department)

Fresh or dried tarragon

Instant espresso powder

Angel food cake

### from your pantry

Olive oil

Salt and pepper

Ground cinnamon

Cayenne pepper

Orange juice

Butter

Chocolate syrup

serves 4

### **before**youstart

Preheat the broiler to cook the chicken.

step 1 — cook the **jasmine rice with shallots**

step 2 — make the **chicken cutlets with pear-applesauce**

step 3 — make the **micro-steamed sugar snap peas and carrots**

step 4 — assemble the **dessert**

step 5 — **serve**

## luckyforyou

Unsweetened applesauce is commonplace on supermarket shelves and that's what you want to use here. Puréed with ripe pears, the just-apple applesauce makes a nicely balanced, tangy-sweet dressing for the chicken, and it's healthier without sugar, of course.

*"I started with foods kids love, and then tweaked them with adult ingredients. The result? A perfect weeknight family dinner."*

—minutemeals' Chef Wendy

## step 1

### cook the **jasmine rice with shallots**

1 large shallot, chopped

1 1/2 teaspoons olive oil

1 cup jasmine rice

1 3/4 cups water

Salt to taste

1. Chop the shallot. In a medium saucepan over medium heat, heat the olive oil. Add the shallot and cook, stirring, 1 minute, until the shallot is nearly tender.

2. Stir in the rice, water, and salt. Bring to a boil over high heat. Reduce the heat to low, cover, and simmer 15 minutes, until the rice is tender and the water has been absorbed. Remove from the heat.

## step 2

### make the **chicken cutlets with pear-applesauce**

Olive oil cooking spray

1 pound skinless boneless chicken breast halves (4 ounces each)

Salt to taste

1/2 teaspoon ground cinnamon

1/4 teaspoon cayenne pepper

2 ripe pears

1 cup unsweetened applesauce

1 tablespoon orange juice

1. Preheat the broiler. Spray a jelly-roll pan with olive oil cooking spray.

2. Season the chicken with salt and sprinkle with the cinnamon and cayenne pepper.

3. Place the chicken on the prepared baking sheet. Broil 5 inches from the heat, turning once, for about 10 minutes or until cooked through. Transfer the chicken to a serving platter and tent loosely to keep warm.

4. While the chicken cooks, core and slice the pears. Place the pear slices, applesauce, and orange juice in a blender. Purée until smooth. Pour into a small serving bowl.

## step 3

### make the **micro-steamed sugar snap peas and carrots**

1 package (12 ounces) stringed sugar snap peas

1 1/2 cups matchstick-cut carrots

2 tablespoons water

1 tablespoon snipped fresh tarragon (or 1 teaspoon dried)

1 teaspoon butter

Salt and pepper to taste

1. Spread the sugar snap peas and carrots in a broad shallow microwave-safe dish. Drizzle with the water and cover with a lid or vented plastic wrap. Microwave on High for 2 to 4 minutes, until the vegetables are crisp-tender.

2. If you are using fresh tarragon, snip enough to measure 1 tablespoon.

Drain the vegetables and place in a serving bowl. Toss the vegetables with the butter. Add the tarragon, salt, and pepper and toss again.

## step 4

### assemble the **angel food cake with chocolate-espresso sauce**

1/4 cup chocolate syrup

1 1/2 teaspoons instant espresso powder

angel food cake 4 slices (1-ounce each)

Combine the syrup and espresso powder in a small bowl, stirring to dissolve. Place 1 piece of angel food cake on each of 4 dessert plates.

## step 5

### serve

1. Spoon some of the pear-applesauce over the chicken and bring the platter to the table. Serve the remaining sauce on the side.

2. Fluff the rice with a fork. Serve the chicken with the rice and sugar snap peas and carrots.

3. When ready for dessert, spoon 1 tablespoon of chocolate sauce over each slice of cake and serve.

---

**Chicken Cutlets with Pear-Applesauce**
Single serving is 1/4 of the total menu

CALORIES 599; PROTEIN 32g; CARBS 99g;
TOTAL FAT 8g; SAT FAT 3g; CHOLESTEROL 70mg;
SODIUM 761mg; FIBER 9g

*12% of calories from fat*

# 1960s aloha chicken

### brown rice with sugar snaps
### romaine salad with blue cheese dressing
### orange wedges & fortune cookies

## shopping list

Sugar snap peas (pretrimmed)

Green pepper

Skinless boneless chicken breast cut for stir-fry

Canned diced tomatoes with green peppers, celery, and onions

Canned sliced water chestnuts

Canned juice-packed pineapple chunks

Sweet-and-sour sauce

Buttermilk

Crumbled blue cheese

Prewashed romaine lettuce

Tomato wedges (from the salad bar)

Radish slices (from the salad bar)

Oranges

Fortune cookies

## from your pantry

10-minute boil-in-bag brown rice

Olive oil

Red wine vinegar

Dijon mustard

Garlic powder

Salt

Freshly ground black pepper

## menu gameplan

serves 4

### beforeyoustart

In a large saucepan, bring the water to a boil, covered, over high heat, to cook the rice.

step **1** cook the **brown rice with sugar snaps**

step **2** cook the **1960s aloha chicken**

step **3** assemble the **romaine salad with blue cheese dressing**

step **4** **serve**

## headsup
To cut a bell pepper into chunks, stand it on a cutting board and slice down the sides to remove the flesh from the core and seeds. Then cut the sides into squares.

*"It's always great to rediscover a childhood favorite. When you can do it without guilt, it's even better."*

—minutemeals' Chef Marge

## step 1

### cook the **brown rice with sugar snaps**

3 quarts water

2 bags (2 cups each) 10-minute boil-in-bag brown rice

2 cups sugar snap peas

1. Bring the water to a boil in a large saucepan, covered, over high heat.

2. Add the rice bags to the boiling water. Cook for 8 minutes.

3. Add the sugar snap peas to the saucepan and boil for 2 minutes, until crisp-tender.

4. Remove the rice bags from the water and let drain. With a slotted spoon, transfer the sugar snap peas to a serving bowl. Open the rice bags and stir the rice into the serving bowl.

## step 2

### cook the **1960s aloha chicken**

1 green pepper, cut into 1-inch chunks

2 teaspoons olive oil

1 pound skinless boneless chicken breast cut for stir-fry

1 can (14 1/2 ounces) diced tomatoes with green pepper, celery, and onions

1 can (8 ounces) sliced water chestnuts, drained

1 can (8 ounces) juice-packed pineapple chunks

3 tablespoons bottled sweet-and-sour sauce

1. Cut the green pepper into 1-inch chunks.

2. Heat the oil in a large nonstick skillet over medium-high heat. Add the green pepper and chicken and cook, stirring frequently, for 3 minutes, until the chicken begins to turn white, but is not cooked through.

3. Meanwhile, drain the tomatoes and water chestnuts.

4. Add the tomatoes, water chestnuts, pineapple and their juice, and sweet-and-sour sauce to the skillet. Bring to a boil, reduce the heat and cook, stirring frequently, for 5 to 8 minutes, or until the chicken is cooked through and the sauce thickens slightly.

## step 3

### assemble the **romaine salad with blue cheese dressing**

1/4 cup buttermilk

1 teaspoon red wine vinegar

1 teaspoon olive oil

1/2 teaspoon Dijon mustard

1/8 teaspoon garlic powder

Salt and freshly ground black pepper to taste

2 tablespoons crumbled blue cheese

1/5 of a 10-ounce bag pre-washed cut up romaine lettuce

8 tomato wedges

1/3 cup radish slices

1. In a small bowl place the buttermilk, vinegar, olive oil, mustard, and garlic powder. Season with salt and pepper. Whisk until blended. Stir in the blue cheese.

2. Arrange the lettuce, tomato wedges, and radish slices in 4 salad bowls. Drizzle some of the blue cheese dressing over each serving, and place the bowls on the table.

## step 4

### serve

1. Turn the aloha chicken onto a deep serving platter and place on the table. Place the rice with sugar snap peas on the table. Serve immediately with the salads.

2. When ready for dessert, cut 4 oranges into wedges and divide among 4 dessert dishes. Serve each with the fortune cookies.

---

**1960s Aloha Chicken**
Single serving is 1/4 of the total menu
CALORIES 575; PROTEIN 34g; CARBS 93g; TOTAL FAT 9g; SAT FAT 2g; CHOLESTEROL 67mg; SODIUM 804mg; FIBER 12g

*14% of calories from fat*

# chicken thighs with kalamata olives and tomatoes

## brown rice
## broccoli with cheese crumbs
## lemon ice

### shopping list

Fresh cilantro

Pitted kalamata olives

Skinless boneless chicken thighs

Canned diced tomatoes with garlic and onion

Broccoli florets (from the salad bar or the produce department)

Lemon ice

### from your pantry

Instant brown rice

Pepper

Extra virgin olive oil

Fat-free reduced-sodium chicken broth

Grated Parmesan cheese

Flavored bread crumbs

**menu gameplan**

serves 4

**step 1** make the **brown rice**

**step 2** make the **chicken thighs with kalamata olives and tomatoes**

**step 3** make the **broccoli with cheese crumbs**

**step 4** **serve**

## headsup
Canned, diced tomatoes are now available with all sorts of seasonings: basil and garlic, Italian herbs, roasted garlic, even green chiles. Any of those flavorings will work here.

*"Chicken thighs have such a rich, meaty flavor. They really stand up to the olives and cilantro here."*

—minutemeals' Chef Marge

## make the **brown rice**

2 cups instant brown rice

Make the rice according to package directions.

## make the **chicken thighs with kalamata olives and tomatoes**

1/2 cup chopped cilantro

1/3 cup pitted kalamata olives (about 2 1/4 ounces)

1 pound skinless boneless chicken thighs

Pepper to taste

2 teaspoons extra virgin olive oil

1 can (14 1/2 ounces) diced tomatoes with garlic and onion

1/2 cup fat-free reduced-sodium chicken broth

1. Chop the cilantro. Coarsely chop the olives.

2. Season the chicken thighs with pepper. In a large nonstick skillet, heat the oil over medium-high heat. Add the chicken thighs to the pan, and cook 6 minutes, turning once, or until both sides are golden.

3. Add the diced tomatoes, chicken broth, cilantro, and olives. Stir to mix. Bring the tomato mixture to a boil. Reduce the heat, cover, leaving the lid slightly ajar, and simmer 8 to 10 minutes, until the chicken is cooked through.

## make the **broccoli with cheese crumbs**

1 pound broccoli florets

Pepper to taste

2 tablespoons grated Parmesan cheese

2 tablespoons flavored bread crumbs

1. Bring 1/2 inch water to a boil in a large skillet, covered, over high heat. Add the broccoli and cook 5 to 7 minutes, until tender.

2. Drain the broccoli and place it in a broad, shallow serving dish. Season with pepper. Scatter the Parmesan cheese and bread crumbs over the broccoli, and place the dish on the table.

## serve

1. Spread the rice on a platter and arrange the chicken thighs on top, spooning the sauce over all.

2. When ready for dessert, serve the lemon ice.

---

**Chicken Thighs with Kalamata Olives and Tomatoes**
**Single serving is 1/4 of the total menu**
CALORIES 557; PROTEIN 33g; CARBS 67g; TOTAL FAT 19g; SAT FAT 4g; CHOLESTEROL 79mg; SODIUM 1098mg; FIBER 7g

*30% of calories from fat*

# thai chicken wraps
## quick vegetable soup
## gingered red cabbage slaw
## tropical fruit sorbet with papaya cubes

menu
**game**plan

serves 4

step **1** cook the **gingered red cabbage slaw**

step **2** make the **thai chicken wraps**

step **3** cook the **quick vegetable soup**

step **4** **serve**

## shopping list

Shredded red cabbage

Pickled (sushi) ginger (jarred or from the seafood department)

Fat-free flour tortillas (8-inch diameter)

Ground chicken or turkey

Scallions

Fresh basil

Baby spinach leaves

Matchstick-cut carrots (from the produce department)

Tropical fruit sorbet

Papaya cubes or pineapple chunks (from the produce department)

## from your pantry

Vegetable oil

Salt and pepper

Sugar

Rice vinegar

Cooking spray

Garlic

Eggs

Lite soy sauce

Ground ginger

Red pepper flakes

Fat-free reduced-sodium vegetable broth

## headsup
If you can't find sushi ginger for the cabbage, grate about 1 tablespoon of fresh ginger and add it to the hot oil with the cabbage.

*"Busy cooks the world over have easy soup-salad-sandwich menus in their repertoire. Here's my Mex-Asian entry."*

—minutemeals' Chef Ruth

## step 1

### cook the **gingered red cabbage slaw**

2 teaspoons vegetable oil

1 bag (8 ounces) shredded red cabbage

Salt and pepper to taste

2 tablespoons water

2 teaspoons sugar

3 tablespoons rice vinegar

2 tablespoons pickled (sushi) ginger

1. Place the oil in a large nonstick skillet over medium heat.

2. Add the cabbage and toss to coat with the oil. Season with salt and pepper. Cook, stirring frequently, about 3 minutes, or until slightly wilted. Add the water, cover, reduce the heat to low, and let steam about 4 minutes, or until the cabbage is crisp-tender. Stir in the sugar and toss for 30 seconds to 1 minute.

3. Remove the cabbage from the heat. Stir in the rice vinegar and pickled ginger.

## step 2

### make the **wraps**

4 fat-free flour tortillas (8-inch diameter)

Cooking spray

1 pound ground chicken or ground turkey

3 scallions

1 large garlic clove

2 large eggs

1½ tablespoons lite soy sauce

½ teaspoon ground ginger

¼ to ½ teaspoon crushed red pepper flakes

About 3 stems fresh basil

1. Turn the oven on to 400°F. Stack the tortillas and wrap in aluminum foil. Place the tortillas in the oven as it heats, 10 to 15 minutes.

2. Coat a large nonstick skillet with cooking spray and place over medium-high heat. Crumble in the chicken or turkey and cook, stirring frequently to break up the lumps, until the pink color is gone, about 5 minutes.

3. Meanwhile, slice the scallions diagonally into ½-inch pieces and mince the garlic. Beat the eggs in a small bowl.

4. Add the scallions, garlic, soy sauce, ginger, and red pepper flakes to the chicken. Cook and stir for 2 minutes. Stir in the beaten eggs and cook, stirring, until set, about 30 seconds. Remove from the heat. Cut the basil into thin slices and stir into the chicken.

## step 3

### cook the **vegetable soup**

1 can (14½ ounces) fat-free reduced-sodium vegetable broth

½ cup water

2 cups prewashed spinach leaves

½ cup matchstick-cut carrots

Pepper to taste

1. Put the broth and water in a medium saucepan. Cover and bring to a boil over high heat.

2. Cut the spinach into slivers.

3. Add the carrots and spinach to the boiling broth. Reduce the heat to medium-low, cover and simmer 3 to 4 minutes, until the vegetables are tender. Season with pepper.

## step 4

### serve

1. Ladle the vegetable soup into small bowls or mugs and serve.

2. Bring the warm tortillas to the table. Transfer the chicken mixture to a serving bowl and place on the table. Assemble wraps, spooning the chicken on one side of a tortilla, folding in the ends, and rolling up.

3. Transfer the slaw to a serving bowl and place on the table.

4. When ready for dessert, place scoops of tropical sorbet in individual dessert dishes. Spoon the papaya cubes or pineapple chunks, about ⅓ cup per serving, next to the sorbet. Place on the table.

---

**Thai Chicken Wraps**
Single serving is ¼ of the total menu
CALORIES 467; PROTEIN 20g; CARBS 70g;
TOTAL FAT 12g; SAT FAT 3g; CHOLESTEROL 183mg;
SODIUM 1078mg; FIBER 5g
*23% of calories from fat*

# broiled chicken sausage

broccoli, pepper, and mushroom toss

texas toasts with garlic

plum compote

## menu gameplan

serves 4

### beforeyoustart

Preheat the broiler to cook the sausages and toasts.

step **1** cook the **broccoli, pepper, and mushroom toss**

step **2** make the **broiled chicken sausage**

step **3** make the **texas toasts with garlic**

step **4** make the **plum compote**

step **5** **serve**

## shopping list

Reduced-fat Italian salad dressing

Package of fully-cooked chicken sausages

Italian bread

Canned pitted purple plums, packed in water

### from the salad bar

Broccoli florets (or from the produce department)

Green and red pepper slices

Onion rings or slices

Mushroom slices (or from the produce department)

Orange slices

## from your pantry

Pepper

Olive oil

Garlic

Sugar

Cinnamon stick

Mustards (variety)

## luckyforyou

All of the produce in the vegetable toss is available, presliced or trimmed, from the salad bar or produce department, saving you chopping and cleanup.

*"It's my job to trim the fat from the old-style dishes my family loves and that's what I did here."*

—minutemeals' Chef Sharon

## step 1
### cook the **broccoli, pepper, and mushroom toss**

3 tablespoons reduced-fat Italian salad dressing

1 cup broccoli florets

1 cup green pepper slices

1 cup red pepper slices

1 cup onion slices

1 cup mushroom slices

Pepper to taste

1. Place the salad dressing in a large, deep, nonstick skillet over medium-high heat.

2. Add the broccoli, pepper slices, onion, and mushroom slices and toss to coat with the dressing.

3. Reduce the heat to medium and cook, stirring occasionally, until the onions and peppers are tender and the broccoli is bright green, about 8 minutes. Season with pepper. Remove from the heat and partially cover to keep warm.

## step 2
### broil the **chicken sausages**

4 fully-cooked chicken sausages

1. Preheat the broiler. Line a broiler pan with aluminum foil. Slice each sausage lengthwise, without cutting all the way through, and open each like a book.

2. Arrange the sausages cut-side up on the broiler pan. Broil 4 to 6 inches from the heat until lightly browned, turning once, about 8 minutes.

## step 3
### make the **texas toasts with garlic**

4 slices (each 1/2 inch thick) crusty Italian bread

2 teaspoons olive oil

1 garlic clove, halved

1. Place the bread slices on a cookie sheet. Broil 4 to 6 inches from the heat, turning once, until crisp and golden.

2. Drizzle a bit of the oil over 1 side of each toast (or brush the oil on with a pastry brush).

3. Rub the oiled sides of the bread with the cut side of the garlic clove. Cut each toast in half.

## step 4
### make the **plum compote**

2 cups pitted canned plums packed in water, drained

1/4 cup water

1/4 cup sugar

2 orange slices

1 cinnamon stick

Drain the plums. In a medium saucepan, stir the water and sugar over medium heat until the sugar is dissolved. Add the plums, the orange slices, and the cinnamon stick and bring to a boil. Reduce the heat and simmer, stirring occasionally, about 5 minutes. Remove from the heat and let stand, partially covered, until ready to serve.

## step 5
### serve

1. Spoon a variety of mustards, such as Dijon, yellow, and spicy brown, into small bowls and place on the table.

2. Divide the broccoli, peppers, and mushrooms among 4 dinner plates. Lay a chicken sausage on top of the vegetables, and place 2 halves of Texas toast on each plate. Serve the sausage and vegetables with 1 teaspoon of mustard per serving.

3. When ready for dessert, divide the warm plums among 4 dessert dishes and spoon the syrup over the top; serve.

---

**Broiled Chicken Sausage**
Single serving is 1/4 of the total menu

CALORIES 406; PROTEIN 21g; CARBS 57g; TOTAL FAT 13g; SAT FAT 3g; CHOLESTEROL 50mg; SODIUM 924mg; FIBER 5g

*27% of calories from fat*

# turkey marsala with mushrooms

## egg noodles primavera
## yogurt with honey and walnuts

serves 4

## shopping list

Egg noodles

Plum tomatoes

Thin-sliced turkey cutlets

Plain low-fat yogurt

Walnuts

### from the salad bar

Broccoli florets (or from the produce department)

Red pepper slices

Mushroom slices (or from the produce department)

## from your pantry

Salt and pepper

Garlic

Olive oil

Fat-free reduced-sodium chicken broth

All-purpose flour

Dry Marsala wine

Honey

## **before**youstart

Bring water to a boil in a large pot, covered, over high heat, to cook the egg noodles.

step **1** cook the **egg noodles primavera**

step **2** cook the **turkey marsala with mushrooms**

step **3** assemble the **yogurt with honey and walnuts**

step **4** **serve**

## headsup

Honey may crystallize over time, especially if stored in the refrigerator. To liquefy it, place the honey in a microwave-safe container, uncovered, and microwave on High, stirring every 15 seconds or so, until liquid; do not boil. Use immediately; the honey will crystallize again as it cools.

*"Veal marsala is classic, but costly. Turkey cutlets are less expensive; the key is cooking them briefly so they stay tender."* —minutemeals' Chef David

## step 1

### cook the **egg noodles primavera**

Salt

8 ounces medium-wide egg noodles

2 cups broccoli florets

1 cup red pepper slices

4 plum tomatoes

2 garlic cloves

1 teaspoon olive oil

2 tablespoons fat-free reduced-sodium chicken broth

1. Bring a large pot of water to a boil, covered, over high heat.

2. Add salt and the egg noodles and cook according to package directions. Add the broccoli and red pepper slices to the pot during the last 3 minutes of cooking. Drain the noodles and vegetables in a colander.

3. While the noodles are cooking, chop the plum tomatoes and the garlic.

4. Heat the olive oil in a large nonstick skillet over medium heat. Add the chopped tomatoes and garlic and cook, stirring, 1 minute. Add the chicken broth and the drained noodles and vegetables to the skillet and toss until heated through. Transfer to a serving bowl and cover to keep warm until serving.

## step 2

### cook the **turkey marsala with mushrooms**

2 garlic cloves

1 pound thin-sliced turkey cutlets

Salt and pepper to taste

1 tablespoon olive oil

8 ounces mushroom slices

1 tablespoon all-purpose flour

1/3 cup dry Marsala wine

1/4 cup fat-free reduced-sodium chicken broth

1. Chop the garlic. Season the turkey cutlets with salt and pepper. Heat 1 1/2 teaspoons of the olive oil in a large nonstick skillet over medium-high heat. Add the turkey cutlets and cook about 2 minutes per side, until lightly browned and just cooked through. Transfer the cutlets to a platter and cover loosely to keep warm.

2. Add the remaining 1 1/2 teaspoons of olive oil to the skillet and stir in the garlic and mushrooms. Sprinkle the flour over and cook, stirring, until the mushrooms are tender, about 3 minutes. Add the Marsala and broth. Increase the heat to high and bring the mixture to a boil. Simmer, stirring often, until slightly thickened. Pour the sauce over the turkey.

## step 3

### assemble the **yogurt with honey and walnuts**

2 cups plain low-fat yogurt

4 tablespoons honey

4 tablespoons chopped walnuts

Divide the yogurt among 4 small bowls and refrigerate until serving.

## step 4

### serve

1. Place a turkey cutlet with some of the Marsala mushroom sauce on each of 4 dinner plates. Add a serving of noodles primavera to each plate.

2. When ready for dessert, top each of the 4 bowls of yogurt with 1 1/2 tablespoons of honey and 1 tablespoon walnuts.

**Turkey Marsala with Mushrooms**
Single serving is 1/4 of the total menu
CALORIES 607; PROTEIN 48g; CARBS 73g;
TOTAL FAT 15g; SAT FAT 3g; CHOLESTEROL 135mg;
SODIUM 517mg; FIBER 5g
*21% of calories from fat*

# turkey cutlets with apricot sauce

## roasted garlic couscous with cherry tomatoes and broccoli

## honeyed ginger plums

### shopping list

Broccoli florets (from the salad bar or the produce department)

Roasted garlic and olive oil couscous

Grape tomatoes

Turkey cutlets

Fresh gingerroot

Dried apricots

Ripe plums

### from your pantry

Fruity olive oil

Olive oil

Salt and pepper

Cornstarch

Apricot preserves

White wine vinegar

Honey

Ground cinnamon

serves 4

### beforeyoustart

Bring the water to a boil in a medium saucepan, covered, over high heat, to cook the couscous. Rinse the plums.

step 1 cook the **couscous**

step 2 cook the **turkey cutlets with apricot sauce**

step 3 prepare the **honeyed plums**

step 4 **serve**

**headsup** Turkey cutlets are available in varying thicknesses. We call for ¼-inch thick cutlets here, and cook them for 8 minutes. If you prefer thin-sliced cutlets, simply cut the cooking time in half.

*"I love the way the grape tomatoes in the couscous stay firm—when you bite into them; they pop a little."*

—minutemeals' Chef Paul

## step 1

### cook the **roasted garlic couscous with cherry tomatoes and broccoli**

12 ounces broccoli florets

1¼ cups plus 3 tablespoons water

1 cup grape tomatoes

1 package (5.8 ounces) roasted garlic and olive oil couscous

1 teaspoon fruity olive oil

1. Spread the broccoli florets in a single layer in a microwave-safe dish with the 3 tablespoons water. Cover with a lid or vented plastic wrap. Microwave on High for 6 to 8 minutes, or until crisp-tender.

2. Bring the remaining 1¼ cups water to a boil in a medium saucepan, covered, over high heat. Stir in the olive oil, the couscous with its seasoning packet, and the grape tomatoes. Cover and let stand 5 minutes. Fluff with a fork, and cover to keep warm until serving.

## step 2

### cook the **turkey cutlets with apricot sauce**

1 teaspoon olive oil

4 turkey cutlets, each ¼ inch thick (about 1¼ pounds total)

Salt and pepper to taste

⅔ cup water

1 teaspoon cornstarch

3 tablespoons apricot preserves

1 tablespoon white wine vinegar

1 teaspoon grated fresh gingerroot

⅓ cup dried apricots (about 10)

1. Place the oil in a nonstick skillet over medium heat. Season the turkey cutlets with salt and pepper. Add the cutlets to the skillet and cook 8 minutes, turning once, until cooked through. Transfer the turkey to a plate and cover loosely with foil.

2. While the turkey cooks, stir together the water, cornstarch, apricot preserves, vinegar, and ginger in a small bowl. Using lightly oiled kitchen scissors, snip strips of apricots into the bowl.

3. Add the apricot mixture to the skillet, place over high heat, and bring to a boil, stirring. Reduce the heat and simmer for 2 minutes or until thickened. Return the cutlets to the pan and spoon the sauce over.

## step 3

### prepare the **honeyed plums**

2 tablespoons honey

⅛ teaspoon ground cinnamon

6 ripe plums

Stir together the honey and cinnamon in a medium bowl. Halve the plums and remove the pits. Cut the plums into wedges and toss with the honey.

## step 4

### serve

1. Fluff the couscous again and divide it among 4 dinner plates. Transfer 1 turkey cutlet to each plate and spoon some of the sauce over.

2. When ready for dessert, toss the plums and spoon into 4 dessert dishes; serve.

---

**Turkey Cutlets with Apricot Sauce**
Single serving is ¼ of the total menu

CALORIES 487; PROTEIN 39g; CARBS 76g; TOTAL FAT 5g; SAT FAT 1g; CHOLESTEROL 82mg; SODIUM 581mg; FIBER 7g

*9% of calories from fat*

# jerk turkey strips
## cool coleslaw
## couscous with dried fruit
## broiled pineapple with lime

## shopping list

Cucumber

Fresh dill

Coleslaw mix

Dried chopped mixed fruit

Couscous

Scallions

Jerk spice blend

Thin-sliced turkey cutlets

Peeled, sliced fresh pineapple (from the salad bar or produce department)

Limes (for juice)

## from your pantry

Low-fat mayonnaise

Cider vinegar

Sugar

Salt

Freshly ground black pepper

Dried oregano

Ground cinnamon

Cooking spray

Lite soy sauce

Brown sugar

serves 4

## **before**youstart

Preheat the broiler for the turkey strips and the pineapple with lime.

step **1** prepare the **cool coleslaw**

step **2** cook the **couscous with dried fruit**

step **3** cook the **jerk turkey strips**

step **4** make the **broiled pineapple with lime**

step **5** **serve**

# heads up

Dried cranberries, cherries, and apricots make pretty alternatives to the prepared dried fruit mix in the couscous. If you buy whole apricots, use lightly oiled kitchen scissors to snip them into small pieces.

*"If you prefer your jerk authentically fiery, add hot sauce to the spice blend, or even a whole hot pepper."*

—minutemeals' Chef David

## step 1

### prepare the **cool coleslaw**

- 1/3 cup low-fat mayonnaise
- 2 tablespoons cider vinegar
- 2 tablespoons sugar
- 2 Kirby cucumbers
- 2 tablespoons snipped fresh dill
- 1 bag (16-ounces) coleslaw mix
- Salt and freshly ground black pepper to taste

1. In a salad bowl stir together the mayonnaise, cider vinegar, and sugar.

2. Chop the cucumbers into small pieces. Snip enough dill to measure 2 tablespoons. Add the cucumbers, dill, and coleslaw mix to the bowl. Toss well to coat and season with salt and pepper. Refrigerate until ready to serve.

## step 2

### cook the **couscous**

- 1 1/3 cups water
- 1 cup chopped, dried mixed fruit
- 1/2 teaspoon dried oregano
- 1/4 teaspoon ground cinnamon
- 1 cup couscous
- 1/8 teaspoon salt
- Freshly ground black pepper to taste

1. Place the water, dried fruit, oregano, and cinnamon in a medium saucepan over medium-high heat. Cover and bring to a boil; boil 1 minute.

2. Remove the saucepan from the heat and stir in the couscous. Cover and let stand 5 minutes. Fluff with a fork, season with salt and pepper, and cover to keep warm until serving.

## step 3

### cook the **jerk turkey**

- Cooking spray
- 4 scallions
- 2 tablespoons cider vinegar
- 1 1/2 tablespoons lite soy sauce
- 2 tablespoons jerk spice blend
- 1 tablespoon sugar
- 1 pound thin-sliced turkey cutlets
- 1/8 teaspoon salt
- Freshly ground pepper to taste

1. Preheat the broiler. Line a baking sheet with aluminum foil and spray foil with cooking spray. Trim the scallions and cut into 1-inch lengths. Place the scallions, cider vinegar, soy sauce, jerk spice blend, and sugar in a blender. Process until mixture is smooth.

2. Cut the turkey cutlets crosswise into 1-inch wide strips. Place in a bowl and pour the jerk mixture over them; sprinkle with the salt and pepper and toss well to coat.

3. Place strips on the prepared baking sheet. Broil 4 inches from the heat, for 3 to 4 minutes per side, or until cooked through. Remove the turkey strips from the oven; leave the broiler on for the pineapple.

## step 4

### make the **broiled pineapple with lime**

- Cooking spray
- 8 slices fresh pineapple, peeled
- 1 tablespoon packed dark brown sugar
- 1 lime, for serving

1. Line a baking sheet with aluminum foil and spray the foil with cooking spray.

2. Arrange the pineapple rings on the prepared baking sheet. Sprinkle with sugar then broil 4-inches from the heat 3 to 4 minutes or until hot and bubbly.

## step 5

### serve

1. Fluff the couscous one more time. Bring the cole slaw to the table. Divide the jerk turkey strips, couscous, and coleslaw among 4 dinner plates.

2. When ready for dessert, arrange 2 pineapple slices on each of 4 dessert plates and squeeze a bit of lime juice over each serving.

**Jerk Turkey Strips**
Single serving is 1/4 of the total menu
CALORIES 617; PROTEIN 38g; CARBS 102g; TOTAL FAT 9g; SAT FAT 2g; CHOLESTEROL 81mg; SODIUM 932mg; FIBER 10g
*12% of calories from fat*

# sonoma turkey burgers

baked potato chips

mustardy red cabbage and broccoli slaw

kirby cucumber spears

icy mocha yogurt frappes

## menu gameplan

## shopping list

Sun-dried tomatoes

Sourdough or potato rolls

Fresh basil leaves

Lean ground turkey (99% fat free)

Goat cheese (optional)

Plain low-fat yogurt

Pre-shredded broccoli slaw

Pre-shredded red cabbage

Vanilla low-fat yogurt

Kirby cucumbers

## from your pantry

Freshly ground black pepper

Smoky barbecue sauce

White vinegar

Onion-flavored or grainy mustard

Sugar

Salt

Low-fat (1%) milk

Unsweetened cocoa powder

Instant espresso or instant coffee powder

serves 4

## beforeyoustart

Bring a small amount of water to boil to soften the sun-dried tomatoes.

step **1** prepare the **sonoma turkey burgers**

step **2** make the **mustardy red cabbage and broccoli slaw**

step **3** prepare the **icy mocha yogurt frappes**

step **4** serve

## luckyforyou

This tangy yogurt-and-mustard dressing makes a healthy alternative to mayonnaise-based dressing. (Low-fat mayonnaise has its uses, but is a bit sweet.) Try it on potato and macaroni salads, adding herbs and seasonings as you wish. If your diet can spare it, add a touch of olive oil to make the sauce a bit "clingier."

*"These burgers were inspired by California cooking. They're light—how many burgers can claim that?—and full of intriguing flavors."*

—minutemeals' Chef Paul

## prepare the **sonoma turkey burgers**

- 3 tablespoons chopped sun-dried tomatoes (not packed in oil)
- 4 sourdough or potato rolls
- 1/4 cup fresh basil leaves
- 1 pound lean ground turkey (99% fat free)
- 3 tablespoons smoky barbecue sauce
- Pepper to taste
- 2 ounces goat cheese (optional)

1. Bring 1 cup or so of water to a boil. Place the sun-dried tomatoes in a small bowl. Add the boiling water to cover. Split the rolls in half. Chop the basil and place in a large bowl.

2. Drain the tomatoes and add to the basil. Season with pepper. Add the ground turkey and the barbecue sauce. Use a fork to stir until combined, and shape into 4 patties, each about 3/4 inch thick.

3. Place a grill pan over medium heat. Add the burgers to the pan and cook for 6 to 7 minutes per side or until cooked through. While the burgers are cooking, spread the bottom side of each roll with 1 tablespoon of the cheese, if using. Place a burger on each bun.

## step 2

## make the **mustardy red cabbage and broccoli slaw**

- 2/3 cup plain low-fat yogurt
- 2 tablespoons white vinegar
- 1 1/2 tablespoons onion-flavored or grainy mustard
- 2 teaspoons sugar
- 1/2 teaspoon salt
- 1 package (8 ounces) pre-shredded broccoli slaw
- 1 package (8 ounces) pre-shredded red cabbage
- Freshly ground black pepper to taste

Whisk together the yogurt, vinegar, mustard, sugar, and salt in a large bowl. Add the broccoli slaw and red cabbage and toss to combine. Season with a generous amount of pepper.

## step 3

## prepare the **icy mocha yogurt frappes**

- 1 1/2 cups low-fat (1%) milk
- 2/3 cup vanilla low-fat yogurt
- 1/4 cup granulated sugar
- 2 tablespoons unsweetened cocoa powder
- 2 teaspoons instant espresso or instant coffee powder
- 12 ice cubes

Place the milk, yogurt, sugar, cocoa, and espresso powder in a blender container and place in the refrigerator. Place 4 tall glasses in the refrigerator.

## step 4

## serve

1. Slice 2 kirby cucumbers into spears and divide them among 4 dinner plates.

2. Place 1 burger on each of the plates. Stir the slaw and spoon next to the burgers. Serve with the baked potato chips.

2. When ready for dessert, add the ice cubes to the milk mixture. Process 1 to 2 minutes, or until smooth and frothy. Divide evenly among the chilled glasses and serve.

---

**Sonoma Turkey Burgers**
Single serving is 1/4 of the total menu
CALORIES 595; PROTEIN 45g; CARBS 90g;
TOTAL FAT 7g; SAT FAT 2g; CHOLESTEROL 83mg;
SODIUM 989mg; FIBER 9g
*10% of calories from fat*

# ground turkey burritos
## with red beans

Mexican rice

burrito fixins'

mandarin orange with passion fruit sorbet

## shopping list

Frozen baby peas

Fat-free flour tortillas
(8-inch diameter)

Canned red kidney beans

Red pepper slices
(from the salad bar)

Ground turkey breast

Salsa verde

Frozen corn kernels

Sweet white onion

Fat-free sour cream

Shredded cabbage

Edy's mandarin orange with
passion fruit sorbet

## from your pantry

Long-grain rice

Tomato paste

Dried oregano

Canola oil

Chili powder

 Fat-free sour cream and flour tortillas, and lean ground turkey make it possible to enjoy this Mexican-style favorite and to stay within the bounds of a healthy menu. If you add burrito fixins' like fat-free cheese or salsa, you'll up the sodium content significantly.

**menu gameplan**

serves 4

step **1** cook the **mexican rice**

step **2** make the **ground turkey burritos with red beans**

step **3** assemble the **burrito fixins'**

step **4** **serve**

*"You don't need to make separate meals to please kids and health-conscious adults. This menu pleases everybody."*

—minutemeals' Chef David

## step 1

### cook the **mexican rice**

3/4 cup frozen baby peas

13/4 cups water

1 cup long-grain rice

1 tablespoon tomato paste

1/2 teaspoon dried oregano

1. Remove the baby peas from the freezer and let stand at room temperature while you cook the rice.

2. Combine the water, rice, tomato paste, and oregano in a microwave-safe dish. Cover with a lid or plastic wrap and microwave on High for 5 minutes. Reduce the power to Medium and cook for 15 minutes longer. Remove the rice from the microwave and stir in the baby peas.

## step 2

### make the **ground turkey burritos with red beans**

4 fat-free flour tortillas (8-inch diameter)

1 can (15 1/2 ounces) red kidney beans

1 cup red pepper slices

2 teaspoons canola oil

12 ounces ground turkey breast

2 teaspoons chili powder

1/2 cup canned or jarred salsa verde

1/2 cup frozen corn kernels

1. Turn the oven to 350°F. Wrap the tortillas in aluminum foil and place them in the oven to warm as it heats, about 15 minutes.

2. Drain and rinse the kidney beans. Chop the red pepper slices.

3. Heat the oil in a large nonstick skillet over medium-high heat. Add the red pepper and cook 1 minute, stirring often. Stir in the turkey and chili powder and cook, stirring and breaking up the turkey, until the pink color is gone, about 5 minutes.

4. Stir in the salsa verde, beans, and corn. Cover and simmer 2 minutes or until hot and bubbly. Remove from the heat and cover to keep warm.

## step 3

### assemble the **burrito fixins'**

1/2 sweet white onion

1 cup fat-free sour cream

1 cup shredded cabbage

Chop the onion. Place the onion, sour cream, and cabbage in small bowls and place on the table with serving spoons.

## step 4

### serve

1. Fluff the rice with a fork and place the dish on the table.

2. Transfer the turkey and bean filling to a serving dish, and place it on the table. Place the hot tortillas on the table. Let everyone fill and roll their own burritos, adding the fixins' they prefer.

3. When ready for dessert, scoop 1/2 cup of sorbet into each of 4 dessert bowls and serve immediately.

**Ground Turkey Burritos**
Single serving is 1/4 of the total menu
CALORIES 721; PROTEIN 28g; CARBS 131g;
TOTAL FAT 10g; SAT FAT 2g; CHOLESTEROL 56mg;
SODIUM 561mg; FIBER 10g

*12% of calories from fat*

# spice-seared duck breasts
## with orange marmalade
### herbed barley
### caraway brussels sprouts
### fresh cherries

## menu gameplan

serves 4

## beforeyoustart

Preheat the oven to 450°F to roast the duck. Rinse and chill the cherries.

**step 1** cook the **herbed barley**

**step 2** cook the **caraway brussels sprouts**

**step 3** cook the **spice-seared duck breasts with orange marmalade**

**step 4** **serve**

## shopping list

Quick-cooking barley

Brussels sprouts

Boneless duck breast halves

Orange marmalade

Cherries

## from your pantry

Fat-free reduced-sodium chicken broth

Dried oregano

Dried thyme

Freshly ground black pepper

Garlic

Salt

Olive oil

Caraway seeds

Paprika

Ground cumin

Ground cinnamon

Ground allspice

## luckyforyou

Contrary to conventional wisdom, duck breasts are amazingly lean—once the skin and underlying layer of fat are removed, that is. To save time ask your butcher to remove the skin and trim the fat for you. The recipe will work beautifully with chicken breasts, too.

*"Duck breasts are party food—which goes to show that party fare doesn't have to be unhealthy or hard to prepare."* —minutemeals' Chef David

## step 1
### cook the **herbed barley**

- 2 cups fat-free reduced-sodium chicken broth
- 1 teaspoon dried oregano
- 1/4 teaspoon dried thyme
- 1 cup quick-cooking barley
- Freshly ground black pepper to taste

Bring the chicken broth, oregano, and thyme to a boil in a medium saucepan, covered, over high heat. Add the barley; cover and reduce the heat to medium-low. Simmer for 10 to 12 minutes or until the barley is tender. Remove from the heat and let stand 5 minutes.

## step 2
### cook the **caraway brussels sprouts**

- 2 cups Brussels sprouts
- 2 garlic cloves
- Salt to taste
- 2 teaspoons olive oil
- 1 teaspoon caraway seeds
- Freshly ground black pepper to taste

**1.** Trim and quarter the Brussels sprouts. Thinly slice the garlic.

**2.** Half-fill a medium saucepan with water, cover, and bring to a boil over high heat. Add the salt and the Brussels sprouts and cook for 5 minutes, until tender. Drain the Brussels sprouts and transfer to a serving bowl. Drape a clean dish towel over the top to keep the sprouts warm.

**3.** Place the oil in a small nonstick skillet over medium-high heat. Add the sliced garlic and caraway seeds. Cook, stirring often, 2 to 3 minutes or until the garlic is lightly browned and tender. Pour the garlic and oil mixture over the sprouts. Season with salt and pepper, and toss to mix. Cover to keep warm.

## step 3
### cook the **spice-seared duck breasts with orange marmalade**

- 1 1/2 teaspoons paprika
- 1 1/2 teaspoons ground cumin
- 1 teaspoon ground cinnamon
- 1/2 teaspoon ground allspice
- 1/4 teaspoon salt
- 1/8 teaspoon freshly ground black pepper
- 4 skinless boneless duck breast halves (4 to 5 ounces each)
- 1 teaspoon olive oil
- 1/4 cup orange marmalade

**1.** Preheat the oven to 450°F.

**2.** Combine the paprika, cumin, cinnamon, allspice, salt, and pepper in a small bowl. Sprinkle mixture over the duck breasts.

**3.** Heat the oil in a large nonstick skillet with an ovenproof handle over medium-high heat. (If the handle on your skillet is not oven-proof, wrap it in aluminum foil.) Add the duck breasts, skinned side down, and cook 2 minutes. Turn and cook 2 minutes longer.

**4.** Remove the skillet from the heat and brush the skinned side of the duck breasts with the marmalade. Transfer the skillet to the oven and roast the duck breasts 6 to 8 minutes for medium.

## step 4
### serve

**1.** Fluff the barley with a fork and season with pepper. Transfer a duck breast to each of 4 dinner plates. Spoon a serving of Brussels sprouts and barley next to each breast, and serve.

**2.** When ready for dessert, place 2 cups cherries in a bowl and serve.

---

Spice-Seared Duck Breasts with Orange Marmalade
Single serving is 1/4 of the total menu
CALORIES 570; PROTEIN 33g; CARBS 96g; TOTAL FAT 10g; SAT FAT 2g; CHOLESTEROL 122mg; SODIUM 726mg; FIBER 13g
*15% of calories from fat*

minute

quick

# meat and meat substitutes

meals
& healthy

# burgers italiano

### skillet red bliss potatoes
### garlicky green beans
### biscotti and fresh or dried figs

## menu
## gameplan

## shopping list

Precut ready-to-cook red bliss potatoes

Extra-lean (93%) ground beef

Roasted red peppers

Ripe tomato

Red onion slices (from the salad bar)

Soft onion rolls

Prewashed spinach leaves (from the salad bar or produce department)

Frozen whole green beans

Fresh or dried figs

Biscotti

## from your pantry

Olive oil

Dried Italian seasoning

Garlic salt

Salt and pepper

Fat-free reduced-sodium chicken broth

Olive oil cooking spray

Grated Parmesan cheese

Day-old bread

Egg

Garlic

Butter

Ketchup or chili sauce

serves 4

## beforeyoustart

Preheat the broiler to cook the burgers. Rinse the figs.

step **1** cook the **skillet red bliss potatoes**

step **2** make the **burgers italiano**

step **3** cook the **garlicky green beans**

step **4** **serve**

## headsup

The burgers will be just as delicious if you substitute ground turkey for the beef.

*"Burgers are so flexible. If you have picky eaters in your house—or burger puritans—don't season their burgers."*

—minutemeals' Chef Patty

## step 1

### cook the **skillet red bliss potatoes**

2 teaspoons olive oil

1 bag (24 ounces) precut ready-to-cook red bliss potatoes

1 teaspoon dried Italian seasoning

1/4 teaspoon garlic salt

1/4 teaspoon pepper

1 can (14 ounces) fat-free reduced-sodium chicken broth

1. Heat the oil in large nonstick skillet over medium-high heat. Add the potatoes, Italian seasoning, garlic salt, and pepper. Cook, shaking the skillet occasionally, until the potatoes are starting to brown, about 7 minutes.

2. Add the chicken broth, reduce the heat to medium and cook, stirring occasionally, for 10 minutes or until the potatoes are tender. Transfer to a serving bowl, cover lightly to keep warm, and place on the table.

## step 2

### make the **burgers italiano**

Olive oil cooking spray

1 pound extra-lean (93%) ground beef

1/2 cup roasted red peppers, drained and chopped

1/4 cup grated Parmesan cheese

1 piece day old bread, crumbled

1 large egg white

1 teaspoon dried Italian seasoning

1 large ripe tomato

Red onion slices

4 soft onion rolls, for serving

8 prewashed spinach leaves, for serving

1. Preheat the broiler. Line a broiler pan with aluminum foil. Spray the broiler-pan rack with the cooking spray.

2. Place the ground beef, roasted peppers, Parmesan cheese, bread, egg white, and Italian seasoning in a medium bowl. Form the mixture into 4 equal-sized, fairly flat patties.

3. Place the patties on the prepared broiler pan and broil 6 inches from the heat for 10 minutes, turning once, until cooked through. Meanwhile, slice the tomato. Arrange the tomato and red onion slices on a small plate, and place on the table.

## step 3

### cook the **garlicky green beans**

1 package (16 ounces) frozen whole green beans

1 small garlic clove, minced

2 teaspoons butter, softened

Salt and pepper to taste

1. Place the green beans in a microwave-safe dish and cook according to the directions on the package. (Or, bring 1 cup of water to a boil in a small saucepan, add the green beans, and cook 3 to 5 minutes, until crisp-tender.) Drain in a colander.

2. Mince the garlic. Combine the butter and garlic in a serving bowl. Add the drained green beans, salt, and pepper and toss to coat. Place the bowl on the table.

## step 4

### serve

1. On 4 dinner plates, pile a few spinach leaves on the bottom halves of each roll. Place a burger on top, and lay the top half of the roll on the dinner plate. Pass the tomato and onion slices, and ketchup or chili sauce for topping.

2. Serve the burgers with the skillet potatoes and the green beans.

3. When ready for dessert, arrange 1 fresh or dried fig and 1 biscotti on each of 4 dessert plates and serve.

**Burgers Italiano**
Single serving is 1/4 of the total menu
CALORIES 730; PROTEIN 40g; CARBS 101g; TOTAL FAT 19g; SAT FAT 7g; CHOLESTEROL 66mg; SODIUM 1,017mg; FIBER 14g
*25% of calories from fat*

# curried beef and chickpeas

## cumin-scented jasmine rice with raisins

## cucumber raita

## bananas with yogurt and 'nilla wafers

serves 4

### shopping list

Frozen chopped spinach

Canned chickpeas

Lean ground beef

Curry paste

Cucumber slices
(from the salad bar)

Shredded carrots
(from the salad bar)

Fresh mint

Plain fat-free yogurt

Bananas

Dannon Light 'n Fit banana
cream yogurt

Reduced-fat 'Nilla wafer
cookies

### from your pantry

Jasmine rice

Golden raisins

Cumin seed or ground cumin

Kosher salt

Onion

Salt

Freshly ground black pepper

**step** 1 cook the **cumin-scented jasmine rice with raisins**

**step** 2 make the **curried beef and chickpeas**

**step** 3 make the **cucumber raita**

**step** 4 **serve**

**headsup** Curry paste, not powder, is what gives this dish its long-simmered flavor. Curry pastes range in spiciness; Thai curry pastes in particular are quite hot, although the Indian curry pastes can be hot, too. If you're not sure how much heat you can take, start with 1 tablespoon, and add more by teaspoons, tasting as you go.

*"If you don't want the bother of cooking rice, just wrap the beef in tortillas or tuck it into pita bread."*

—minutemeals' Chef Sharon

## step 1

### cook the **cumin-scented jasmine rice with raisins**

2 cups water

1 cup jasmine rice

2 tablespoons golden raisins

1 teaspoon cumin seeds, or 1/2 teaspoon ground cumin

1/2 teaspoon kosher salt

**1.** Place the water, rice, raisins, cumin seeds or ground cumin, and salt in a heavy medium saucepan. Bring to a boil over high heat.

**2.** Cover the saucepan, reduce the heat to low, and cook the rice very gently until all the water has been absorbed and the rice is tender, about 15 minutes.

## step 2

### make the **curried beef and chickpeas**

1 package (10 ounces) frozen chopped spinach

1 can (15 ounces) chickpeas, rinsed and drained

1 medium onion

12 ounces lean ground beef

1 to 3 tablespoons curry paste

1/2 cup water

Salt to taste

**1.** Unwrap the spinach. Place in a glass pie plate and microwave on High for 3 minutes, until thawed. Drain in a colander and press out the excess water. Drain and rinse the chickpeas. Chop the onion.

**2.** Place the ground beef and onion in a large nonstick skillet over medium-high heat. Cook, stirring often, until the beef is lightly browned, about 6 minutes.

**3.** Drain the beef in a colander and return to the skillet. Add the chickpeas and spinach to the skillet. Stir in the curry paste and water. Reduce the heat and simmer for 2 minutes to blend the flavors.

## step 3

### make the **cucumber raita**

3 cups cucumber slices

1/2 cup shredded carrots

2 tablespoons snipped fresh mint leaves

1/2 cup plain fat-free yogurt

Salt and freshly ground black pepper

Coarsely chop the cucumber slices. Place the cucumber, carrots, and mint in a medium salad bowl. Stir in the yogurt and season with salt and pepper. Place the raita on the table.

## step 4

### serve

**1.** Divide the rice among 4 dinner plates. Spoon the curried beef and chickpeas next to the rice. Serve with the raita, spooning it over the meat and rice.

**2.** When ready for dessert, slice one small banana into each of 4 small serving bowls. Spoon half of a 6-ounce container of banana cream yogurt over each serving, and serve each with 2 vanilla wafers.

**Curried Beef and Chickpeas**
Single serving is 1/4 of total menu

CALORIES 501; PROTEIN 28g; CARBS 84g; TOTAL FAT 7g; SAT FAT 2g; CHOLESTEROL 40mg; SODIUM 728mg; FIBER 9g

*12% of calories from fat*

# beef and green bean stir-fry
## white rice
## melon with minted balsamic vinegar
## pear or apple sorbet

**menu**
**game**plan

serves 4

step **1** make the **white rice**

step **2** make the **melon with minted balsamic vinegar**

step **3** make the **beef and green bean stir-fry**

step **4** **serve**

## shopping list

Honeydew or cantaloupe chunks (from the salad bar)

Fresh gingerroot

Beef strips cut for stir-fry

Green beans

Canned water chestnuts

Pear or apple sorbet

## from your pantry

White rice

Balsamic vinegar

Brown sugar

Dried mint

Salt

Freshly ground black pepper

Lite soy sauce

Cornstarch

Toasted sesame oil

Canola oil

Fat-free reduced-sodium beef broth

## headsup
If you use high-quality balsamic vinegar, you may not need to add brown sugar to the melon salad. If, however, your balsamic vinegar is quite acidic, sweeten it with a pinch of brown sugar whenever you use it, whether in sweet or savory dishes.

*"Stir-frying is an easy way to add vitamins and fiber to dinner. Load up on vegetables, and limit the meat."*

—minutemeals' Chef Wendy

## step 1

### make the **white rice**

- 2 cups water
- 1 cup white rice

Make the rice according to package directions.

## step 2

### make the **melon with minted balsamic vinegar**

- 4 cups cubed honeydew or cantaloupe melon chunks
- 2 tablespoons balsamic vinegar
- 1 teaspoon packed brown sugar
- 1/2 teaspoon dried mint
- Salt and freshly ground black pepper to taste

In a serving bowl, toss the melon with the vinegar, brown sugar, and mint. Season with salt and pepper. Divide the melon among 4 small bowls.

## step 3

### make the **beef and green bean stir-fry**

- 1/4 cup lite soy sauce
- 2 tablespoons cornstarch
- 2 teaspoons minced fresh ginger
- 1/2 teaspoon toasted sesame oil
- 12 ounces beef strips cut for stir-fry
- 1 pound green beans, trimmed and cut into 2-inch pieces
- 4 teaspoons canola oil
- 1 can (8 ounces) sliced water chestnuts, drained
- 1/2 cup fat-free reduced-sodium beef broth

**1.** In a medium bowl, stir together the soy sauce, cornstarch, ginger, and sesame oil. Add the beef to the marinade and toss to mix. Trim the green beans and cut into 2-inch pieces.

**2.** Heat 2 teaspoons of the canola oil over medium-high heat in a large nonstick wok or large deep skillet. Add the green beans and stir-fry for 2 to 3 minutes, or until slightly tender. Transfer the beans to a bowl.

**3.** Add the remaining 2 teaspoons oil to the wok or skillet and heat. Increase the heat to high, and add the beef, reserving the marinade, and water chestnuts and stir-fry for 1 to 2 minutes, or until the beef is no longer pink.

**4.** Add the reserved marinade, the beef broth, and the green beans to the skillet. Reduce the heat to medium and simmer 2 minutes, stirring often, until the sauce is thickened and glossy.

## step 4

### serve

**1.** Spread the rice on a platter, mounding it slightly at the sides. Spoon the beef and green bean stir-fry into the middle of the rice. Serve with the melon.

**2.** When ready for dessert, scoop the sorbet into bowls and serve.

---

**Beef and Green Bean Stir-Fry**
Single serving is 1/4 of the total menu
CALORIES 588; PROTEIN 29g; CARBS 96g;
TOTAL FAT 11g; SAT FAT 2g; CHOLESTEROL 56mg;
SODIUM 835mg; FIBER 7g
*16% of calories from fat*

# steak with horseradish sauce

micro-baked potatoes

zucchini with red peppers and dill

malted milk

## menu gameplan

## shopping list

Boneless beef for London broil (sirloin, top round, or flank steak)

Reduced-fat sour cream

Fat-free half-and-half

Prepared horseradish sauce

Baked potatoes

Zucchini

Red pepper slices (from the salad bar)

Fresh dill

Malted milk powder

## from your pantry

Salt

Freshly ground black pepper

Olive oil

Milk, skim-plus or low-fat (1%)

serves 4

## beforeyoustart

Preheat the broiler to cook the steak.

step 1 make the **steak with horseradish sauce**

step 2 make the **micro-baked potatoes**

step 3 steam the **zucchini with red peppers and dill**

step 4 make the **malted milk**

step 5 **serve**

## headsup

Unless your diet precludes salt, it's likely that you use it, and pepper, in virtually everything you cook. Here's a handy way to keep both seasonings at your fingertips: Combine about 2 parts pepper and 1 part salt in a custard cup to keep on your counter.

*"I don't want my family to feel deprived. This meat-and-potatoes menu satisfies everybody, and it's healthy, too."*

—minutemeals' Chef **Wendy**

step 1

## make the **steak with horseradish sauce**

1 pound boneless beef for London broil (sirloin, top round, or flank steak)

Salt and freshly ground black pepper to taste

1/4 cup reduced-fat sour cream

2 tablespoons fat-free half-and-half

1 tablespoon prepared horseradish sauce

**1.** Turn on the broiler. Line a broiler pan with aluminum foil. Season the steak with salt and pepper. Place the steak on the broiler-pan rack and broil 5 inches from the heat for 15 minutes, turning once, for medium-rare. Transfer the steak to a cutting board and tent with foil to keep warm.

**2.** Meanwhile, in a small serving bowl combine the sour cream, half-and-half, and horseradish sauce.

step 2

## make the **micro-baked potatoes**

4 baking potatoes (about 8 ounces each)

Pierce each potato several times with a fork. Arrange them in a spoke-like fashion in the microwave. Microwave on High for 14 to 16 minutes, until tender.

step 3

## steam the **zucchini with red peppers and dill**

2 small zucchini (about 6 ounces each), trimmed and sliced

1/2 cup red pepper slices

2 teaspoons olive oil

2 teaspoons snipped fresh dill

Salt and pepper to taste

**1.** Place a collapsible vegetable steamer in a large pot, add 1 inch water, cover, and bring to a boil over high heat.

**2.** Trim the zucchini and slice into thin rounds, about 1/4 inch thick. Coarsely chop the pepper slices. Add the zucchini and peppers to the steamer basket, cover, and steam for 3 to 4 minutes, until the zucchini is tender. Transfer to a serving bowl and toss with the olive oil. Snip about 2 teaspoons fresh dill over the zucchini, season with salt and pepper, and toss again. Place the bowl on the table.

step 4

## make the **malted milk**

3/4 cup malted milk powder

1 quart chilled skim plus or low-fat (1%) milk

In a pitcher mix the malted milk powder with the milk until dissolved. Chill until ready to serve.

step 5

## serve

**1.** Slice the steak very thinly on the diagonal, across the grain. Divide the slices among 4 dinner plates

**2.** Place a baked potato on each plate, and spoon the horseradish sauce over the steak and potatoes. Add a serving of zucchini to each plate.

**3.** When ready for dessert, pour the malted milk into 4 tall glasses and serve with straws.

---

**Steak with Horseradish Sauce**
Single serving is 1/4 of total menu, using top sirloin steak

CALORIES 620; PROTEIN 45g; CARBS 80g; TOTAL FAT 13g; SAT FAT 6g; CHOLESTEROL 91mg; SODIUM 613mg; FIBER 7g

*19% of calories from fat*

# teriyaki flank steak
## sesame-scallion rice
## vegetable stir-fry
## fresh orange wedges

## shopping list

Fresh gingerroot

Garlic

Lemon (for juice)

Hoisin sauce

Flank steak

Chopped scallions
(from the salad bar)

Fresh broccoli stir-fry mix

Peanut satay sauce

Oranges

## from your pantry

Cooking spray

Lite soy sauce

Rice vinegar

10-minute boil-in-bag
brown rice

Sesame seeds

Toasted sesame oil

Salt

luckyforyou The ingredients that give
this meal its Asian flair no
longer require a separate trip to a specialty store. Rice
vinegar, hoisin sauce, lite soy sauce, toasted sesame oil,
and satay sauce (you can substitute a peanutty stir-fry
sauce) are most likely near one another in the Oriental/Asian
ingredient aisle of your supermarket.

## menu
## gameplan

serves 4

## beforeyoustart
Preheat the broiler. Bring the water to a
boil in a large pot, covered, over high
heat, to cook the rice.

step 1 cook the **teriyaki flank steak**

step 2 cook the **sesame-scallion rice**

step 3 cook the **vegetable stir-fry**

step 4 **serve**

*"A well-stocked pantry makes this meal easy. If yours isn't, buy a few favorites, and go from there."*

—minutemeals' Chef Sarah

## step 1
### cook the **teriyaki flank steak**

Cooking spray

1-inch piece fresh gingerroot, peeled

2 large garlic cloves, peeled

1 tablespoon lemon juice (1 lemon)

1/2 cup hoisin sauce

1 tablespoon lite soy sauce

1 tablespoon rice vinegar

1 flank steak (1 1/2 pounds), trimmed

1. Preheat the broiler. Line a broiler pan with foil. Spray the broiler pan rack with cooking spray.

2. Peel the ginger and garlic. Squeeze 1 tablespoon juice from the lemon. In food processor or mini-chopper, finely chop the ginger and garlic. Add the hoisin sauce, lemon juice, soy sauce, and rice vinegar. Pulse until blended.

3. Place the flank steak in a shallow baking dish and pour the marinade over. Turn to coat and let marinate 3 minutes.

4. Place the flank steak on the prepared broiler pan. Broil about 4 inches from the heat, 5 to 7 minutes per side for medium-rare. Spoon any marinade remaining in the baking dish over the steak as it's broiling. Transfer the steak to a cutting board.

## step 2
### cook the **sesame-scallion rice**

2 bags (2 cup size) 10-minute boil-in-bag brown rice

2 tablespoons sesame seeds

1/2 cup chopped scallions

1/2 teaspoon toasted sesame oil

1/2 teaspoon salt

1. Cook the rice in boiling water according to the directions on the package.

2. Place the sesame seeds on a microwave-proof plate and microwave on High until lightly toasted, stirring halfway through, for 2 to 3 minutes. Carefully tip the seeds onto a plate to cool.

3. Remove the bags of cooked rice and pour out the water in the pot. Combine the scallions and sesame oil in the rice pot. Stir over medium heat for 1 minute, or until the scallions wilt. Stir in the rice, toasted sesame seeds, and salt.

## step 3
### cook the **vegetable stir-fry**

1 bag (1 pound) broccoli stir-fry mix

2 tablespoons peanut satay sauce

1. Cook the broccoli stir-fry mix according to the directions on the bag.

2. Transfer the vegetables to a serving dish and toss with the satay sauce. Place the dish on the table.

## step 4
### serve

1. Thinly slice the flank steak on the diagonal across the grain. Divide the slices among 4 dinner plates.

2. Turn the rice into a serving dish and place on the table. Serve the rice and stir-fry vegetables with the steak.

3. When ready for dessert, cut 4 oranges into wedges and place on 4 dessert plates.

---

**Teriyaki Flank Steak**
Single serving is 1/4 of total menu

CALORIES 590; PROTEIN 42g; CARBS 71g;
TOTAL FAT 18g; SAT FAT 6g; CHOLESTEROL 74mg;
SODIUM 705mg; FIBER 11g

*26% of calories from fat*

# spicy thai beef strips
## on crisp salad
### warm flour tortillas
### fresh papaya wedges

## menu gameplan

serves 4

### beforeyoustart
Preheat the broiler to cook the beef strips.

step 1 cook the **spicy thai beef strips**

step 2 prepare the **warm flour tortillas**

step 3 assemble the **crisp salad**

step 4 prepare the **fresh papaya wedges**

step 5 **serve**

### shopping list

Boneless beef top round steak

Cilantro

Limes (for juice and wedges)

Chinese chili paste with garlic

Fat-free flour tortillas (10-inch diameter)

Prewashed colorful crisp mixed salad greens

Cucumber slices (from the salad bar)

Red onion slices (from the salad bar)

Large ripe papaya

### from your pantry

Nonstick vegetable cooking spray

Garlic

Salt

Lite soy sauce

Sugar

Vegetable oil

## luckyforyou
Because these beef strips are cut so thin, they cook in all of 2 minutes! As for the papaya: Look for papayas the size of a large mango. When ripe, the skin is a deep golden, and the flesh gives slightly when pressed. The seeds, which clump together in the center of the fruit, are edible, so scoop some into a bowl and let your diners taste a few.

*"Want this even faster? Skip the salad and serve the beef strips wrapped in large Boston or iceberg lettuce leaves."* —minutemeals' Chef Hillary

### step 1

## cook the **spicy thai beef strips**

Nonstick vegetable cooking spray

1 pound boneless beef top round steak

1/2 cup cilantro sprigs

4 garlic cloves

2 tablespoons fresh lime juice (2 limes)

1 tablespoon water

1 tablespoon Chinese chili paste with garlic, or less to taste

1/2 teaspoon salt

1. Preheat the broiler. Line a broiler pan with aluminum foil. Spray the broiler-pan rack with nonstick vegetable cooking spray.

2. Trim any fat from the steak. Cut the steak in half lengthwise, then cut across the grain into 1/8-inch-thick strips.

3. In a food processor, put the cilantro, garlic, lime juice, water, chili paste, and salt. Process to a smooth paste, adding a little more water if necessary. Scrape into a large bowl. Add the steak strips and toss to coat. Marinate for 2 minutes.

4. Arrange the steak strips in a single layer on the prepared pan rack. Broil 2 to 3 inches from the heat for 1 minute on each side for medium rare, or to desired doneness. Remove from the broiler and transfer the strips to a bowl.

### step 2

## prepare the **warm flour tortillas**

4 fat-free flour tortillas (10-inch diameter)

Wrap the stack of tortillas loosely in aluminum foil and heat them in a toaster oven at 350°F for 5 to 8 minutes. Transfer to a napkin-lined basket and cover to keep warm. Place the basket on the table.

### step 3

## assemble the **crisp salad**

1 bag (5 ounces) prewashed colorful crisp mixed salad greens

1 1/2 cups cucumber slices

1/2 cup red onion slices

1/4 cup fresh lime juice (3 or 4 large limes)

1 tablespoon lite soy sauce

2 teaspoons sugar

1 tablespoon vegetable oil

1. In a large salad bowl, combine the greens, cucumbers, and red onion slices.

2. In a small bowl, stir together the lime juice, soy sauce, sugar, and vegetable oil until the sugar is dissolved. Pour the dressing over the salad and toss.

### step 4

## prepare the **fresh papaya wedges**

1 large ripe papaya

1 lime, cut in wedges

Halve the papaya. Scoop out the seeds and place in a small bowl or discard. Slice each half in half again. Place one papaya quarter on each of 4 dessert plates. Cut the lime into wedges and place a wedge on each plate.

### step 5

## serve

1. Top the salad with the steak strips, adding any juices that have accumulated in the bowl. Toss well and divide the beef and salad evenly among 4 dinner plates. Serve with the warm tortillas.

2. When ready for dessert, serve the papaya with spoons for scooping, letting diners squeeze lime juice over the papaya if they wish. Pass the seeds, if desired.

**Spicy Thai Beef Strips**
Single serving is 1/4 of total menu

CALORIES 383; PROTEIN 31g; CARBS 44g; TOTAL FAT 10g; SAT FAT 3g; CHOLESTEROL 75mg; SODIUM 689mg; FIBER 4g

*23% of calories from fat*

# pepper-and-fennel beef tenderloin

## smashed creamers with yogurt and chives

## roasted green beans

## pears with vanilla frozen yogurt and maple syrup

### shopping list

Green beans

Creamers or small Yukon Gold potatoes

Fresh chives

Plain low-fat yogurt

Boneless beef tenderloin steaks

Canned pear halves, packed in juice or extra-lite syrup

Vanilla frozen yogurt

### from your pantry

Olive oil

Salt

Freshly ground black pepper

Fat-free reduced-sodium chicken broth

Cracked black peppercorns

Fennel seeds

Coarse salt

Maple syrup

serves 4

## beforeyoustart

Preheat the oven to 450°F to roast the green beans. Rinse the pears.

step **1** cook the **roasted green beans**

step **2** make the **smashed creamers with yogurt and chives**

step **3** cook the **pepper-and fennel-crusted beef tenderloin**

step **4** serve

## headsup
Fennel seeds make a crunchy, aromatic crust for the beef tenderloin. Don't buy more than you will use in 6 months; as with all seeds and dried herbs, the flavor fades over time.

*"This is the perfect meal for a harried holiday host. It's elegant, it's extravagant, and it's easy."*

—minutemeals' Chef David

## step 1

### cook the **roasted green beans**

1 pound green beans

1 1/2 teaspoons olive oil

Salt and freshly ground black pepper to taste

**1.** Preheat the oven to 450°F. Trim the ends of the green beans.

**2.** On a jelly-roll pan, toss the green beans with the olive oil and salt and pepper.

**3.** Roast the green beans, giving the pan a good shake once or twice during roasting, for 10 minutes, or until crisp-tender.

## step 2

### make the **smashed creamers with yogurt and chives**

1 pound creamers or small Yukon Gold potatoes

2 tablespoons snipped chives

1/2 cup fat-free reduced-sodium chicken broth

1/4 cup plain low-fat yogurt

1/2 teaspoon salt

Freshly ground black pepper to taste

**1.** If the potatoes are quite small, halve them; if larger, quarter them.

**2.** Put the potatoes in a medium saucepan and add water to cover. Cover and bring to a boil over high heat. Uncover and simmer until tender when tested with a fork, about 12 minutes. Snip enough chives to measure 2 tablespoons.

**3.** Drain the potatoes in a colander. Place the broth in the potato-cooking saucepan over high heat. When it boils, reduce the heat to low and return the potatoes to the saucepan. Using a potato masher, roughly smash the potatoes; they should be very chunky. Remove the pan from the heat and beat in the chives, yogurt, salt, and pepper. Cover and keep warm.

## step 3

### cook the **pepper-and-fennel beef tenderloin**

2 teaspoons cracked black pepper

1 1/2 teaspoons fennel seeds

1/2 teaspoon coarse salt

4 boneless beef tenderloin steaks, each 4 ounces and 1/2-inch thick

1 teaspoon olive oil

**1.** Combine the cracked black pepper-corns, fennel seeds, and salt in a small bowl. Press mixture onto both sides of each steak.

**2.** Heat the oil in a large heavy skillet over medium-high heat. Add the steaks and cook 3 to 4 minutes per side for medium rare. Transfer each steak to a dinner plate.

## step 4

### serve

**1.** Place a steak on each of 4 dinner plates. Add a serving of smashed creamers and roasted green beans to each plate, and bring to the table.

**2.** When ready for dessert, thinly slice each of 4 pear halves and fan on a dessert plate. Place 1/2 cup vanilla frozen yogurt at the edge of the fan, and drizzle 2 teaspoons of maple syrup over the yogurt and pears. Serve.

---

**Pepper-and-Fennel Beef Tenderloin**
Single serving is 1/4 of the total menu

CALORIES 487; PROTEIN 34g; CARBS 59g; TOTAL FAT 13g; SAT FAT 5g; CHOLESTEROL 77mg; SODIUM 788mg; FIBER 7g

*24% of calories from fat*

# caribbean pork tenderloin with peach salsa

minted bulgur pilaf
french-cut green beans
pineapple fruit-juice bars

serves 4

## shopping list

Small pork tenderloin

Small red onion

Jerk seasoning

Scallions

Bulgur

Dried currants

Fresh mint

Sliced canned peaches, packed in juice

Lime (for juice)

Frozen French-cut green beans

Pineapple fruit-juice bars

## from your pantry

Cooking spray

Fat-free reduced-sodium chicken broth

Ground allspice

Salt and pepper

Honey

## menu gameplan

**before**youstart

Bring the chicken broth and water to a boil in a medium saucepan, covered.

step **1** cook the **pork tenderloin**

step **2** cook the **minted bulgur pilaf**

step **3** cook the **french-cut green beans**

step **4** make the **peach salsa**

step **5** serve

## headsup

Many of the mixed spice blends sold in supermarkets contain salt; check the ingredient list on the packaging. If there is salt in the jerk spice blend you are using, use less or no salt to season the pork tenderloin, and simply pass salt at the table.

*"Double the pork and use the extra for sandwiches. Dab some sharp mustard on the bread—it's perfect with the salsa."* —minutemeals' Chef Paul

### step 1
## cook the **pork tenderloin**

1 small pork tenderloin, about 1 pound

1 small red onion

Cooking spray

1¹/2 teaspoons jerk seasoning

**1.** Cut the pork crosswise into eight 1-inch-thick slices. Peel the onion, leaving the root end intact. Cut the onion into 8 wedges. Spray a grill pan with cooking spray and place over medium heat. Sprinkle both sides of pork with jerk seasoning.

**2.** Place the pork and onions in the grill pan. Cook the onions for 8 minutes, turning once. Cook the pork for 8 to 12 minutes, turning once, until the slices are a bit pink in the center and still juicy. Transfer the slices to a plate and tent with aluminum foil.

### step 2
## cook the **minted bulgur pilaf**

1 cup fat-free, reduced-sodium chicken broth

³/4 cup water

2 scallions

1 cup bulgur

2 tablespoons dried currants

¹/4 teaspoon ground allspice

1 tablespoon chopped fresh mint

Salt and pepper to taste

**1.** Place the broth and water in a medium saucepan, cover, and bring to a boil over high heat. Slice the scallions.

**2.** Add the scallions, bulgur, currants, and allspice to the broth. Return to a boil, reduce the heat, cover, and simmer for 8 minutes or until the liquid is absorbed and the bulgur is tender.

**3.** While the bulgur is cooking, chop enough mint to measure 1 tablespoon. Remove the bulgur from the heat, and stir in the mint and salt and pepper. Cover to keep warm until serving.

### step 3
## cook the **french-cut green beans**

1 package (10 ounces) frozen French-cut green beans

Salt and pepper to taste

Cook the green beans according to the directions on the package. Transfer to a serving bowl and season with salt and pepper.

### step 4
## make the **peach salsa**

1 can (15 ounces) sliced peaches, packed in juice

1 tablespoon honey

1 tablespoon fresh lime juice

1¹/2 teaspoons jerk seasoning

8 grilled onion wedges

Drain the peaches. Cut the slices into chunks and place in a medium bowl. Add the honey, lime juice, and remaining 1¹/2 teaspoons jerk seasoning. When the grilled onion wedges are cool enough to handle, coarsely chop and add to peach mixture. Toss to combine and set the bowl on the table.

### step 5
## serve

**1.** Place 2 pieces of pork on each of 4 dinner plates. Spoon some of the peach salsa over the pork.

**2.** Spoon some of the minted bulgur and green beans onto the plates. Serve.

**3.** When ready for dessert, serve the pineapple fruit-juice bars.

**Caribbean Pork Tenderloin with Peach Salsa**
Single serving is ¹/4 of the total menu
CALORIES 416; PROTEIN 32g; CARBS 65g;
TOTAL FAT 5g; SAT FAT 2g; CHOLESTEROL 67mg;
SODIUM 730mg; FIBER 10g
*10% of calories from fat*

# wasabi pork tenderloin

## gingered jasmine rice
## broccoli-basil slaw
## raspberry coolers

menu
gameplan

### shopping list

Fresh gingerroot

Scallions

Fresh basil

Broccoli slaw (from the produce department)

Pork tenderloin

Wasabi powder

Bananas

Frozen unsweetened raspberries

### from your pantry

Jasmine rice

Salt

Teriyaki sauce

Fat-free mayonnaise

Freshly ground black pepper

Cooking spray

Brown sugar

Skim milk

Frozen orange juice concentrate

serves 4

### **before**youstart

Preheat the broiler to cook the pork. Bring the water to a boil.

step 1 — cook the **gingered jasmine rice**

step 2 — make the **broccoli-basil slaw**

step 3 — cook the **wasabi pork tenderloin**

step 4 — assemble the **raspberry coolers**

step 5 — **serve**

## heads up

Powdered wasabi, the bright green Japanese horseradish so hot it can bring tears to your eyes, is now available on the spice rack in the baking aisle. Don't limit its use to Japanese-style dishes: Use it as a seasoning on broiled fish or chicken, in potato salad, or sprinkled over rice.

*"Broiling brings out the full flavor of meat, so you don't need to make a fancy sauce."*

—minutemeals' Chef Lisa

## step 1
### cook the **gingered jasmine rice**

2 cups water

1 cup jasmine rice

2 slices unpeeled fresh gingerroot, each about the size of a quarter

Salt to taste

2 scallions

Bring the water to a boil in a medium saucepan, covered, over high heat. Stir in the rice and gingerroot slices. Return to a boil, cover, reduce the heat, and simmer the rice very gently until all the water has been absorbed, and the rice is tender, about 15 minutes. Chop the scallions.

## step 2
### make the **broccoli-basil slaw**

1 cup loosely packed fresh basil leaves, thinly sliced

3 tablespoons teriyaki sauce

2 tablespoons fat-free mayonnaise

1 package (12 ounces) broccoli slaw

Freshly ground black pepper to taste

**1.** Thinly slice the basil.

**2.** In a salad bowl, with a fork, mix the teriyaki sauce and mayonnaise. Add the broccoli slaw, basil, and pepper to taste. Toss to coat the broccoli slaw. Place the slaw on the table.

## step 3
### cook the **wasabi pork tenderloin**

Cooking spray

1 pork tenderloin, about 1 pound

Salt to taste

2 tablespoons wasabi powder

2 tablespoons packed brown sugar

**1.** Preheat the broiler. Line a broiler pan with aluminum foil. Spray the broiler pan rack with cooking spray.

**2.** Cut the pork tenderloin on an angle into $1/2$-inch-thick slices. Place the pork slices on the prepared broiler pan. Season on both side with the salt.

**3.** In a small bowl stir together the wasabi powder and brown sugar. Sprinkle the mixture on both sides of the pork.

**4.** Broil the pork 6 inches from the heat for about 5 minutes, turning once, until pork is firm and still a touch pink inside and juicy.

## step 4
### assemble the **raspberry coolers**

2 cups skim milk

2 medium bananas, cut into chunks

1 cup frozen unsweetened raspberries

$1/4$ cup frozen orange juice concentrate

Place the ingredients for the raspberry coolers in the blender, and set in the freezer until ready for dessert.

## step 5
### serve

**1.** Fluff the rice with a fork and discard the ginger slices. Stir in the chopped scallions and spoon the rice into a serving dish.

**2.** Divide the pork slices among 4 plates. Serve with the rice and the broccoli slaw.

**3.** When ready for dessert, whirl the coolers in the blender until smooth, and serve in tall glasses with straws.

---

**Wasabi Pork Tenderloin**
Single serving is $1/4$ of the total menu

CALORIES 532; PROTEIN 37g; CARBS 86g;
TOTAL FAT 5g; SAT FAT 2g; CHOLESTEROL 69mg;
SODIUM 1009mg; FIBER 9g

*9% of calories from fat*

# pork chops with apples and onions
## herbed barley
## crudite
## warmed jam-glazed grapefruit halves

menu
**game**plan

serves 4

## shopping list

Quick-cooking barley

Fresh chives, optional

Firm red-skinned apples

Boneless center-cut pork loin chops

Grapefruits

### from the salad bar

Onion slices

Cauliflower florets (4 ounces)

Cherry tomatoes (1 pint)

Carrot and celery sticks
(4 ounces each)

## from your pantry

Dried fines herbes or herbes de Provence

Salt and pepper

Dried thyme

Cooking spray

Canola oil

Cider vinegar

Ground cumin

Seedless raspberry preserve

### **before**youstart

Bring the water to a boil in a medium saucepan, covered, over high heat, to cook the barley. Preheat the broiler.

step **1** cook the **herbed barley**

step **2** cook the **pork chops with apples and onions**

step **3** prepare the **warmed jam-glazed grape-fruit halves**

step **4** **serve**

luckyforyou Quick-cooking barley, with a cooking time reduced to 10 minutes from 45 minutes for regular barley, is a snap to use in soup, salad, or pilaf. And a ½-cup serving of cooked pearl barley contains 3 grams of fiber—about 6 times more than the ½ gram in a serving of long-grain white rice.

*"Something wonderful happens to apples and onions when they cook together. They get sweet, and are especially lovely with pork."*

—minutemeals' Chef Ruth

## step 1

### cook the **herbed barley**

2 cups water

1 cup quick-cooking barley

1 teaspoon dried fines herbes or herbes de Provence

Salt and pepper to taste

2 tablespoons snipped fresh chives, optional

Place 2 cups water in a medium saucepan. Cover and bring to a boil over high heat. Stir in the barley, dried herbs, and salt. Cover, reduce the heat to low, and simmer for 10 minutes, or until tender. Remove from the heat and let stand for 5 minutes. Snip in enough chives to measure 2 tablespoons, if using. Season with pepper, fluff with a fork, and cover to keep warm.

## step 2

### cook the **pork chops with apples and onions**

2 firm red-skinned apples

4 boneless center-cut loin pork chops, each 4 ounces, trimmed

1/2 teaspoon dried thyme

Salt and pepper

Cooking spray

2 teaspoons canola oil

1 cup onion slices

1/4 cup cider vinegar

1/2 cup water

1 teaspoon ground cumin

1. Core the apples; do not peel. Halve the apples through the core end and thinly slice crosswise.

2. Season the pork chops with thyme, salt, and pepper. Lightly coat a large heavy skillet with cooking spray. Place the skillet over high heat and add the chops. Cook the chops for 4 minutes, until brown; turn and cook 2 minutes more, or until the chops are browned and just a bit pink in the center. Transfer the chops to a plate and cover with foil to keep warm.

3. Add the oil and onion slices to the hot skillet. Reduce the heat to medium. Cook and stir the onion for 3 minutes or until starting to soften. Stir in the vinegar, water, cumin, and apples. Season with salt and pepper. Bring to a boil, reduce the heat to low, cover, and simmer for 3 minutes, or until the apples are tender.

## step 3

### prepare the **warm jam-glazed grapefuit halves**

2 small pink grapefruits

2 tablespoons seedless raspberry preserves

1. Preheat the broiler. Halve the grapefruits. Cut between the segments, if desired.

2. Spread the raspberry preserves on the grapefuit halves. Broil about 6 to 8 inches from the heat until the preserves just begin to bubble, about 5 minutes.

## step 4

### serve

1. Arrange the cauliflower florets, cherry tomatoes, and carrot and celery sticks on a platter. Place the platter on the table.

2. Place 1 chop on each of 4 dinner plates. Spoon the apple and onion mixture over, dividing evenly. Transfer the barley pilaf to a serving dish.

3. When ready for dessert, place a grapefruit half on each of 4 serving dishes. Place on the table.

---

**Pork Chops with Apples and Onions**
Single serving is 1/4 of total menu
CALORIES 528; PROTEIN 31g; CARBS 67g;
TOTAL FAT 17g; SAT FAT 5g; CHOLESTEROL 70mg;
SODIUM 407mg; FIBER 11g
*29% of calories from fat*

# souvlaki pork
## with creamy feta sauce
### sweet 'n tangy cucumber salad
### pita bread
### grape ice and purple grapes

## shopping list

Shaved ice (from the supermarket fish counter)

Frozen grape concentrate

Lemons

Boneless pork chops

Crumbled feta cheese

Reduced-fat Ranch dressing

Plain fat-free yogurt

Scallions

Cucumber slices (from the salad bar)

Pita breads (6-inch diameter)

Purple grapes

## from your pantry

Garlic

Onion

Dried oregano

Dried mint

Ground allspice

Salt and pepper

White vinegar

Sugar

serves 4

## beforeyoustart

Rinse and chill the purple grapes.

| step | 1 | make the **grape ice** |
|------|---|-------------------------|
| step | 2 | cook the **souvlaki pork with creamy feta sauce** |
| step | 3 | make the **sweet 'n tangy cucumber salad** |
| step | 4 | **serve** |

## headsup

The ice recipe is limited only by what juice concentrates you find in your grocer's freezer. Try it with lemon, limeade, pineapple, or orange juice concentrate, or a mixture of cranberry and orange.

*"Kids and adults love the souvlaki. If your kids aren't fans of feta cheese, use Ranch dressing on their sandwiches."* —minutemeals' Chef Paul

## make the **grape ice**

3 cups shaved ice

1 can (12 ounces) frozen grape concentrate

1. Put the shaved ice and grape concentrate in a food processor. Pulse to mix.

2. Transfer the mixture to a metal bowl, cover with aluminum foil, and place in the freezer.

## step 2

## cook the **souvlaki pork with creamy feta sauce**

2 lemons

2 garlic cloves

1 onion

3 boneless pork chops ($3/4$ pound), $1/2$-inch thick

$3/4$ teaspoon dried oregano

$1/2$ teaspoon dried mint

$1/4$ teaspoon ground allspice

$1/4$ teaspoon salt

$1/4$ teaspoon pepper

3 tablespoons feta cheese crumbles

2 tablespoons reduced-fat Ranch salad dressing

2 tablespoons plain fat-free yogurt

1. Grate 2 teaspoons zest from 1 of the lemons. Cut the other lemon into wedges. Finely chop the garlic to measure 2 teaspoons. Cut the onion into thick slices.

2. Place the pork, onion slices, oregano, mint, allspice, salt, pepper, $1^1/2$ teaspoons of the garlic, and 1 teaspoon of lemon zest in a medium bowl. Toss until the pork is evenly coated.

3. Heat a grill pan over medium heat or coat a large nonstick skillet with olive oil spray. Add the pork and onion slices to the pan and grill for 7 to 9 minutes, turning once, until the pork is juicy and just slightly pink in the center and onions are tender. Remove from the heat.

4. While the pork cooks, in a small bowl mash the feta cheese with a fork. Stir in the Ranch dressing, yogurt, and the remaining 1 teaspoon lemon zest and $1/2$ teaspoon garlic. Place the bowl on the table.

5. Cut the pork into thin slices and place in a bowl with the grilled onion.

## step 3

## make the **sweet 'n tangy cucumber salad**

2 scallions

$1/4$ cup white vinegar

3 tablespoons water

2 tablespoons sugar

$1/4$ teaspoon salt

$1/8$ teaspoon pepper

1 pound cucumber slices

Chop the scallions and place in a medium salad bowl. Add the vinegar, water, sugar, salt, and pepper and stir to dissolve the sugar. Add the cucumber slices and toss to mix. Place the bowl on the table.

## step 4

## serve

1. Cut four 6-inch pita breads in half. Place 2 halves on each of 4 dinner plates. Place a lemon wedge on each plate, for squeezing over the souvlaki.

2. Place the souvlaki on the table and serve with the feta sauce and cucumber salad. (The meat may either be spooned into the pita breads or served separately, with the sauce spooned over the top.)

3. When ready for dessert, scoop the grape ice into 4 dessert dishes and serve with the purple grapes.

---

**Souvlaki Pork with Creamy Feta Sauce**
Single serving is $1/4$ of total menu

CALORIES 682; PROTEIN 32g; CARBS 118g; TOTAL FAT 13g; SAT FAT 4g; CHOLESTEROL 60mg; SODIUM 830mg; FIBER 16g

*16% of calories from fat*

# sweet and spicy pork chops

### honeyed sweet potatoes
### oniony kale
### fruit compote with yogurt

menu
gameplan

## shopping list

Mixed chopped dried fruit

Canned juice-packed sliced peaches

Orange (for zest)

Plain low-fat yogurt

Sweet potatoes

Pumpkin pie spice

Frozen chopped kale

Frozen chopped onions

Lemon pepper no-salt seasoning

Boneless pork loin chops

## from your pantry

Brown sugar

Cinnamon stick

Honey

Salt

Olive oil

Cumin

Garlic powder

Ground ginger

Cayenne pepper

Canola oil

serves 4

## beforeyoustart

Bring 1 inch of water to a boil in a large saucepan with a steamer insert.

step **1** make the **fruit compote with yogurt**

step **2** cook the **honeyed sweet potatoes**

step **3** make the **oniony kale**

step **4** prepare the **sweet and spicy pork chops**

step **5** **serve**

luckyforyou Kale, a member of the cabbage family, is rich in vitamins A and C, and a good source of phytochemicals, thought to be helpful in cancer prevention.

*"Fruit, spices, and a touch of sweetness create a cool-weather menu—real rib-sticking food that's healthy, too."*

—minutemeals' Chef Marge

## step 1

### make the **fruit compote with yogurt**

1 package (5 ounces) mixed chopped dried fruit

1 can (15¼ ounces) juice-packed peach slices

1 orange

1 tablespoon brown sugar

1 cinnamon stick

¼ cup plain low-fat yogurt

1. Place the dried fruit in a medium saucepan. Drain the juice from the peaches into the saucepan. Using a vegetable peeler, remove a strip of peel from the orange and add it to the fruit and juice along with the brown sugar and cinnamon stick.

2. Bring the mixture to a boil over high heat. Cover, reduce the heat, and simmer 10 to 15 minutes, until the fruit is tender. Remove the saucepan from the heat and stir in the sliced peaches. Partially cover the saucepan to keep the compote warm until serving.

## step 2

### cook the **honeyed sweet potatoes**

3 small sweet potatoes, about 1¼ pounds

2 tablespoons honey

½ teaspoon pumpkin pie spice

¼ teaspoon salt

1. Peel the potatoes and cut lengthwise into ½-inch-thick slices. Place the slices in a steamer basket and arrange the basket over boiling water. Cover and steam for 10 to 12 minutes, or until fork-tender.

2. Scoop out about ½ cup of the steaming liquid and drain the sweet potatoes. Return the sweet potatoes to the saucepan and stir in the honey, pumpkin pie spice, and salt. Cover to keep warm.

## step 3

### make the **oniony kale**

1 package (10 ounces) frozen chopped kale

¾ cup frozen chopped onions

2 tablespoons water

1½ teaspoons lemon pepper no-salt seasoning

1 teaspoon olive oil

½ teaspoon salt

Place the kale and chopped onions in a microwave-safe dish and sprinkle with water. Cover with a lid or vented plastic wrap. Microwave on High for 10 to 12 minutes, stirring after 5 to 6 minutes. Drain, if necessary, and transfer to a serving bowl. Stir in the lemon-pepper seasoning, olive oil, and salt.

## step 4

### prepare the **pork chops**

1 tablespoon packed brown sugar

1 teaspoon cumin

¼ teaspoon garlic powder

¼ teaspoon ground ginger

¼ teaspoon salt

⅛ teaspoon cayenne pepper

4 boneless pork loin chops, each 4 ounces

1 teaspoon canola oil

1. In a small bowl, combine the brown sugar, cumin, garlic powder, ginger, salt, and cayenne pepper. Sprinkle the spice mixture evenly over both sides of the pork chops, and gently press it in.

2. Heat the oil in a large nonstick skillet over medium heat. Add the pork chops and cook for 6 to 8 minutes, turning once, or until pork is just slightly pink in the center.

## step 5

### serve

1. Coarsely mash the sweet potatoes in the pan, adding ⅓ to ½ cup of the reserved cooking liquid to make chunky mashed potatoes.

2. Place 1 pork chop on each of 4 dinner plates, and spoon some potatoes and kale alongside.

3. When ready for dessert, spoon the warm compote into 4 dessert dishes, and top each with 1 tablespoon of yogurt.

---

**Sweet and Spicy Pork Chops**
Single serving is ¼ of the total menu

CALORIES 604; PROTEIN 33g; CARBS 94g;
TOTAL FAT 13g; SAT FAT 4g; CHOLESTEROL 70mg;
SODIUM 691mg; FIBER 9g

*19% of calories from fat*

# lamb kabobs
## with lemon and garlic
### basmati rice with currants
### cucumber salad
### dried apricots and almonds

**menu**
**gameplan**

## shopping list

Basmati rice

Currants

Red pepper

Small zucchini

Vidalia onion

Lemons (for juice)

Lamb cubes for kabobs,
preferably cut from the leg

Large cucumber

Scallion

Plain low-fat yogurt

Plum tomato

Dried apricots

Whole almonds

## from your pantry

Curry powder

Salt

Cooking spray

Olive oil

Garlic

Ground cumin

Cayenne pepper

Freshly ground black pepper

Rice vinegar

Dried mint

serves 4

## **before**youstart

Bring 2 cups water of water to a boil in
a medium saucepan, covered. Preheat
the broiler for the lamb kabobs.

step **1** cook the **basmati rice with currants**

step **2** cook the **lamb kabobs with lemon and garlic**

step **3** assemble the **cucumber salad**

step **4** **serve**

## headsup
If you thread the lamb cubes
somewhat loosely on the
skewers they will cook faster than if they are pressed
together. Cubes cut from the leg should be lean, but if the
cubes are fatty, trim them before broiling so that the flavorful pan juices will be almost fat-free. Then you can
pour them over the cooked kabobs without skimming.

*"I'm hooked on basmati rice. It's got that wonderful, nutty flavor, and some brands cook in just 10 minutes."*

—minutemeals' Chef Sarah

## cook the **basmati rice with currants**

2 cups water

1 cup basmati rice

3 tablespoons currants

1 teaspoon curry powder

1/2 teaspoon salt

1. Bring the water to a boil in a medium saucepan, covered, over high heat.

2. Stir in the rice, currants, curry powder, and salt. Bring to a boil; reduce the heat and simmer, covered, 10 to 15 minutes or according to package directions.

### step 2

## cook the **lamb kabobs with lemon and garlic**

Cooking spray

1 small red pepper, cut into 1-inch cubes

1 small zucchini, cut into 1/2-inch thick slices

1/2 Vidalia onion, cut into wedges

2 tablespoons lemon juice

1 tablespoon olive oil

1 large garlic clove, crushed through a press

1/4 teaspoon ground cumin

1/8 to 1/4 teaspoon cayenne pepper

Salt and freshly ground pepper to taste

1 pound lamb cubes for kabobs (1 1/4-inch cubes)

1. Preheat the broiler. Line a broiler pan with aluminum foil and spray the broiler pan rack with cooking spray.

2. Cut the red pepper into cubes. Trim and slice the zucchini. Cut the onion into wedges through the root end.

3. In a bowl, combine 1 tablespoon of the lemon juice and the olive oil. Crush the garlic into the bowl. Stir in the cumin, cayenne pepper, salt, and black pepper. Add lamb cubes and toss to coat well.

4. Thread the lamb cubes on 4 skewers. Arrange the lamb skewers on prepared broiler-pan rack. Scatter vegetables around the lamb and sprinkle the remaining lemon juice and salt and pepper.

5. Broil lamb and vegetables for 5 minutes. Stir the vegetables and turn the kabobs. Broil 3 to 5 minutes longer or until the lamb is medium rare.

### step 3

## assemble the **cucumber salad**

1 hothouse cucumber

1 scallion, sliced

1 tablespoon rice vinegar

Salt and freshly ground pepper to taste

2 tablespoons plain low-fat yogurt

1 tablespoon water

1 small garlic clove, crushed through a press

1/4 teaspoon dried mint

1 plum tomato, diced

1. Cut the cucumber in quarters lengthwise. Cut the quarters cross-wise into 3/4-inch cubes. Slice the scallion.

2. Place the cucumber and scallion on a serving plate. Sprinkle with the vinegar and season with salt and pepper.

3. In a small cup, combine the yogurt, water, garlic, and mint. Season with salt and pepper. Stir well and drizzle over the cucumber. Dice the tomato and sprinkle on top. Place the salad on the table.

### step 4

## serve

1. Divide the rice among 4 dinner plates. Place a skewer of lamb on top of each serving. Spoon the vegetables into a serving bowl and place on the table.

2. When ready for dessert, arrange 1/4 cup dried apricots and 2 tablespoons almonds on each of 4 dessert plates.

---

**Lamb Kabobs with Lemon and Garlic**
Single serving is 1/4 of total menu

CALORIES 564; PROTEIN 28g; CARBS 82g; TOTAL FAT 18g; SAT FAT 3g; CHOLESTEROL 56mg; SODIUM 806mg; FIBER 9g

*27% of calories from fat*

# simple broiled lamb steak

### buttermilk mashed potatoes
### green beans with basil
### ripe peaches or nectarines

## shopping list

Red potatoes

Buttermilk

Boneless lamb steak

Green beans

Fresh basil

Peaches

## from your pantry

Garlic

Salt

Freshly ground black pepper

Cooking spray

Dijon mustard

Worcestershire sauce

Extra virgin olive oil

serves 4

## beforeyoustart

Bring the water to a boil in a medium saucepan, covered. Preheat the broiler to cook the lamb.

step 1   cook the **buttermilk mashed potatoes**

step 2   cook the **simple broiled lamb steak**

step 3   cook the **green beans with basil**

step 4   **serve**

## headsup
Lamb steak is usually cut from the leg, a lean part of the lamb. Like lean beef steak, lamb steak is best cooked medium-rare; longer cooking will make it tough. You can substitute shoulder steaks, but they contain quite a bit of fat and some bone. If you do use them, buy double the amount called for here and trim all the fat before broiling.

*"Each dish in this menu is clean and simple—not 1 recipe has more than 5 ingredients."*

—minutemeals' Chef Marge

## step 1
### cook the **buttermilk mashed potatoes**

1¼ pounds red potatoes, cut into 1-inch chunks

2 garlic cloves, sliced

1¼ teaspoons salt

½ cup buttermilk

⅛ teaspoon freshly ground black pepper

**1.** Bring 3 cups water to a boil in a medium saucepan, covered, over high heat.

**2.** Cut the potatoes into 1-inch chunks. Slice the garlic.

**3.** Add the potatoes, garlic, and 1 teaspoon salt to the boiling water. Reduce the heat to medium, cover, and simmer 15 minutes, or until the potatoes are tender.

**4.** Drain the potatoes and garlic in a colander. Return the hot potatoes to the saucepan. With a potato masher, mash the potatoes to a chunky texture. Gradually add the buttermilk, mashing the potatoes until creamy.

**5.** Stir in the remaining ¼ teaspoon salt and season with freshly ground black pepper.

## step 2
### cook the **simple broiled lamb steak**

Cooking spray

1 garlic clove, minced

2 teaspoons Dijon mustard

2 teaspoons Worcestershire sauce

1¼ pounds lean boneless lamb steak, about 1-inch thick

⅛ teaspoon freshly ground black pepper

**1.** Preheat the broiler. Line a broiler pan with aluminum foil. Spray a broiler-pan rack with cooking spray.

**2.** Mince the garlic. Combine the garlic, mustard, and Worcestershire sauce in a pie plate; stir until blended. Add the lamb steak and turn to coat. Let marinate for 5 minutes.

**3.** Place the lamb steak on the prepared broiler pan. Broil the lamb 3 to 5 inches from the heat, for 4 minutes. Turn the steak. Spread the lamb with any marinade remaining in the dish. Broil the lamb 3 to 5 minutes longer for medium-rare. Sprinkle the lamb with the pepper and transfer to a carving board.

## step 3
### cook the **green beans**

1 pound green beans, trimmed

2 tablespoons water

1 tablespoon fresh basil

1 teaspoon extra virgin olive oil

⅛ teaspoon salt

**1.** Trim the green beans and place them in a microwave-safe dish. Sprinkle with the water. Cover with vented plastic wrap or a lid, and microwave on High for 2 to 3 minutes, until crisp-tender.

**2.** If necessary, drain any water from the green beans. Add the olive oil, basil, and salt, and toss to mix.

## step 4
### serve

**1.** Cut the lamb across the grain on a slight diagonal into thin (¼-inch) slices. Arrange on 4 dinner plates and spoon any juices from the pan or carving board over each serving.

**2.** Place the mashed potatoes and green beans in 4 serving dishes and place on the table.

**3.** When ready for dessert, serve the peaches or nectarines.

**Simple Broiled Lamb Steak**
Single serving is ¼ of total menu

CALORIES 378; PROTEIN 32g; CARBS 40g; TOTAL FAT 10g; SAT FAT 3g; CHOLESTEROL 82mg; SODIUM 556mg; FIBER 8g

*24% of calories from fat*

# bbq tvp
## on whole-grain buns

potato and green bean salad with buttermilk dressing

cherry tomatoes

applesauce and cookies

**menu**
**gameplan**

serves 4

step **1** cook the **bbq tvp**

step **2** make the **salad**

step **3** **serve**

### shopping list

Sweet onion, such as Vidalia

Textured vegetable protein

Whole-grain hamburger buns

Precut potatoes

Pretrimmed green beans

Red onion slices
(from the salad bar)

Low-fat buttermilk

Cherry tomatoes (from
the salad bar or produce
department)

Applesauce (no sugar added,
16-ounce jar)

Oatmeal raisin cookies,
such as Archway brand
(1 per person)

### from your pantry

Canola oil

Ketchup

Spicy brown mustard

Molasses

Worcestershire sauce

Garlic powder

Ground ginger

Light mayonnaise

Red wine vinegar

Caraway seeds

Ground cumin

Ground cinnamon

## headsup
Textured vegetable protein (also called textured soy protein) is made from defatted soy flour that is processed into granules. Its texture—somewhere between ground beef and coarse grains—makes it a popular vegetarian alternative to ground beef. A healthy one, too: a half cup (cooked) serving has 24 grams of protein, less than 1 gram of fat, and no cholesterol.

*"Meat and potatoes? Not quite—but barbecued TVP is a fool-proof way to work soy into your kids' diet."*

—minutemeals' Chef Marge

## step 1

### cook the **bbq tvp**

1 teaspoon canola oil

1/2 sweet onion, thinly sliced

3/4 cup plus 2 tablespoons ketchup

1 cup water

2 tablespoons spicy brown mustard

1 tablespoon molasses

2 teaspoons Worcestershire sauce

1 teaspoon garlic powder

1/2 teaspoon ground ginger

1 cup textured vegetable protein

4 whole-grain hamburger buns

**1.** Heat the oil in a medium nonstick skillet over medium-high heat. Slice the onion. Add the onion to the skillet and cook, stirring occasionally, until tender, about 3 minutes.

**2.** Stir in the ketchup, water, mustard, molasses, Worcestershire sauce, garlic powder, and ginger and bring to a boil. Cover, reduce the heat to medium, and simmer for 5 minutes.

**3.** Stir in the textured vegetable protein, cover, and simmer, stirring occasionally, until the vegetable protein is softened, about 8 minutes. If the mixture is too thick, add a bit more water.

**4.** Meanwhile, split the hamburger buns. Place the halves in a toaster oven and toast until lightly colored.

## step 2

### make the **salad**

1 bag (16 ounces) precut potatoes

1/4 pound pretrimmed fresh green beans

1/2 cup red onion slices

1/4 cup low-fat buttermilk

2 tablespoons light mayonnaise

1 to 2 tablespoons red wine vinegar

1 1/2 teaspoons caraway seeds

1/2 teaspoon ground cumin

**1.** Place the potatoes in a large saucepan, add enough cold water to cover them by 1 inch, and bring to a boil over high heat. Boil until tender when tested with a fork, 8 to 10 minutes.

**2.** Add the green beans to the pan for the last 2 minutes of cooking time. Drain immediately. Transfer the vegetables to a medium shallow salad bowl and add the onion slices.

**3.** While the potatoes are cooking, whisk together the buttermilk, mayonnaise, vinegar, caraway seeds, and cumin until combined. Pour the dressing over the still-warm vegetables and toss gently to combine. Let stand at room temperature.

## step 3

### serve

**1.** Place the cherry tomatoes in a bowl and bring the bowl to the table.

**2.** Place the bottom half of a hamburger bun on each of 4 dinner plates. Spoon about 1/2 cup of the sloppy Joe mixture over each, and top with the remaining halves. Serve immediately with the potato and green bean salad and the cherry tomatoes.

**3.** When ready for dessert, spoon 1/2 cup applesauce into each dessert bowl, sprinkle with cinnamon, and garnish each with an oatmeal raisin cookie.

---

**BBQ TVP on Whole-Grain Buns**
Single serving is 1/4 of the total menu
CALORIES 499; PROTEIN 20g; CARBS 95g;
TOTAL FAT 9g; SAT FAT 2g; CHOLESTEROL 8mg;
SODIUM 1063mg; FIBER 13g

*15% of calories from fat*

# broccoli and tofu stir-fry

### spiced melon salad
### cherry sundaes
### brown rice

## shopping list

Oyster sauce

Roasted garlic in purée

Enriched firm tofu

Broccoli florets (from the produce department)

Grape tomatoes

Fresh basil

Cantaloupe chunks (from the salad bar or produce department)

Lime (for juice)

Fresh mint or cilantro

Dried cherries

Cherry jam

Vanilla fat-free frozen yogurt

## from your pantry

Instant brown rice

White wine vinegar

Mild Louisiana-style cayenne pepper sauce

Olive oil

Ground coriander

Ground cumin

Salt

Pepper

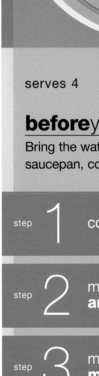

serves 4

## **before**youstart

Bring the water to a boil in a medium saucepan, covered.

step **1** cook the **brown rice**

step **2** make the **broccoli and tofu stir-fry**

step **3** make the **spiced melon salad**

step **4** start the **cherry sundaes**

step **5** **serve**

## heads up

Enriched tofu has about half the calories and less fat than regular tofu. It does, however, contain more sodium: a 3-ounce serving of enriched tofu contains 30 milligrams of sodium, while the same-size serving of regular contains none.

*"The combination of vegetables in the stir-fry makes it chunky, so the sauce has lots of surface to cling to."*

—minutemeals' Chef Paul

### step 1

## cook the **brown rice**

2 cups instant brown rice

Prepare the rice according to package directions.

### step 2

## make the **broccoli and tofu stir-fry**

2 tablespoons white wine vinegar

2 tablespoons oyster sauce

2 tablespoons water

1 tablespoon mild Louisiana-style cayenne pepper sauce

1 teaspoon roasted garlic in purée

12 ounces enriched firm tofu

1 teaspoon olive oil

12 ounces (1 bag) broccoli florets

1 container (10 ounces) grape tomatoes

1/4 cup chopped fresh basil

**1.** Combine the vinegar, oyster sauce, water, pepper sauce, and garlic in a medium bowl. Cut the tofu into 3/4-inch pieces and add with the sauce mixture. Mix until tofu is well coated.

**2.** Heat the olive oil in a large non-stick skillet over medium-high heat. Add the broccoli and stir-fry for 6 minutes, until crisp-tender. Add the grape tomatoes and stir-fry 1 minute more, until tomatoes are heated. Stir in the tofu and the

sauce mixture; cook, stirring often, for 2 minutes more, until heated through.

**3.** Remove the skillet from the heat and cover to keep warm. Chop enough basil to measure 1/4 cup.

### step 3

## make the **spice melon salad**

1 to 1 1/4 pounds cantaloupe chunks

1 tablespoon lime juice

1/8 teaspoon ground coriander

1/8 teaspoon ground cumin

1/8 teaspoon pepper

1/8 teaspoon salt

1 tablespoon chopped fresh mint or cilantro

**1.** Place the cantaloupe chunks in a serving bowl.

**2.** Squeeze 1 tablespoon of juice from the lime. Add the lime juice, coriander, cumin, salt, and pepper to the cantaloupe and toss. Snip 1 tablespoon of mint or cilantro over the melon and toss again. Place the bowl on the table.

### step 4

## start the **cherry sundaes**

1/3 cup dried cherries

Water

1/3 cup cherry jam or preserves

2 cups vanilla fat-free frozen yogurt

Place the cherries in a small dish. Add water to cover and microwave on high for 30 seconds. Remove from the oven and set aside to let the cherries soften. Spoon the jam in a microwave-safe liquid measuring cup.

### step 5

## serve

**1.** Fluff the rice with a fork and divide among 4 dinner plates or shallow bowls.

**2.** Add the basil to the stir-fry and toss. Spoon the stir-fry mixture over the rice, dividing evenly.

**3.** When ready for dessert, drain the cherries in a small strainer and stir into the jam. Microwave on high for 30 seconds. Scoop the frozen yogurt into dessert dishes and spoon the cherry sauce on top. Serve at once.

---

**Broccoli and Tofu Stir-Fry**
Single serving is 1/4 of the total menu
CALORIES 559; PROTEIN 19g; CARBS 114g;
TOTAL FAT 4g; SAT FAT 0g; CHOLESTEROL 2mg;
SODIUM 430mg; FIBER 8g
*6% of calories from fat*

minute

quick

# fish and seafood

meals & healthy

# lemon-pepper cod
## on lightly dressed greens
### cumin-scented rice
### ginger-poached pears

menu
**gameplan**

serves 4

**shopping list**

Gingerroot

Bosc pears

Lemons (for juice)

Salad greens
(from the salad bar)

Cod fillets

**from your pantry**

Sugar

Onion

Olive oil

Ground cumin

Long-grain rice

Low-fat vinaigrette dressing

Lemon pepper

Dry white wine

step **1** make the **ginger-poached pears**

step **2** cook the **cumin-scented rice**

step **3** prepare the **lightly dressed greens**

step **4** cook the **lemon-pepper cod**

step **5** **serve**

**heads**up  For most people, fish is cooked through when it flakes in the thickest part when tested with a fork. If you like fish a bit more moist, cook it 1 minute less than the suggested cooking time.

*"If you use the freshest fish you can and fresh lemon juice, you can't go wrong here."*

—minutemeals' Chef Marge

## step 1
## make the **ginger-poached pears**

3 tablespoons chopped gingerroot

2 ripe Bosc pears

1 lemon

3/4 cup water

1/3 cup sugar

1. Chop enough ginger to measure 3 tablespoons. Peel, halve, and core the pears. Squeeze 1 tablespoon juice from the lemon.

2. In a medium saucepan, combine the water, sugar, ginger, and lemon juice and bring to a boil over high heat, stirring to dissolve the sugar. Add the pears. Cover and simmer over low heat, turning occasionally, until the pears are tender, about 15 minutes. Let stand in the syrup until serving time.

## step 2
## cook the **cumin-scented rice**

1 small onion

1 tablespoon olive oil

1 tablespoon ground cumin

1 1/2 cups long-grain rice

2 1/2 cups water

1. Finely chop the onion.

2. Combine the onion and olive oil in a medium saucepan and sauté, stirring, for 3 minutes, until soft-ened. Stir in the cumin and cook for 30 seconds.

3. Add the rice and water, stir, and reduce the heat to low. Cover and simmer for 15 minutes, until the liquid is absorbed.

## step 3
## prepare the **lightly dressed greens**

2 cups salad greens

2 tablespoons low-fat vinaigrette dressing

Place the salad greens in a bowl, add the vinaigrette, and toss. Dividing the greens equally, place a serving on each of 4 dessert plates.

## step 4
## cook the **lemon-pepper cod**

4 cod fillets, each 3/4 to 1 inch thick (1 1/4 pounds total weight)

1 teaspoon lemon pepper

1 teaspoon olive oil

1/3 cup dry white wine

1 tablespoon lemon juice

1. Rinse the cod fillets and pat dry. Sprinkle the lemon pepper on both sides of the fillets and pat it on.

2. In a large nonstick skillet, heat the olive oil over medium-high heat until hot. Add the cod fillets in 1 layer and cook about 4 minutes per side, or until golden and cooked through when tested with a fork. Remove to a plate and keep warm.

3. Squeeze 1 tablespoon juice from the lemon. Increase the heat to high and add the wine and lemon juice to the skillet. Cook for 3 or 4 minutes, until slightly thickened.

## step 5
## serve

1. Top the greens on each plate with a cod fillet and drizzle some of the lemon sauce over each serving.

2. Fluff the rice with a fork. Add a serving of rice to each plate and serve.

3. When ready for dessert, spoon a pear half into each dessert bowl, being sure to include some of the cooking syrup and ginger.

**Lemon-Pepper Cod on Lightly Dressed Greens**
Single serving is 1/4 of the total menu
CALORIES 538; PROTEIN 23g; CARBS 95g;
TOTAL FAT 7g; SAT FAT 1g; CHOLESTEROL 37mg;
SODIUM 201mg; FIBER 4g
*12% of calories from fat*

# flounder fillets
## with mustard, capers, and fennel seed
### baby carrots with fresh dill
### quick slaw
### caramel pudding

**menu gameplan**

serves 4

**before**youstart

Preheat the oven to 425°F.

| step | 1 | roast the **baby carrots with fresh dill** |
| step | 2 | bake the **flounder fillets with mustard, capers, and fennel** |
| step | 3 | make the **caramel pudding** |
| step | 4 | prepare the **quick slaw** |
| step | 5 | **serve** |

## shopping list

Baby carrots

Fresh dill

Flounder fillets

Capers

Pre-shredded green cabbage or coleslaw mix

## from your pantry

Olive oil

Salt

Country-style Dijon mustard

Freshly ground black pepper

Fennel seeds

Dry white wine

Dark brown sugar

Cornstarch

Low-fat (2%) milk

Rice vinegar

Sugar

**heads**up When the oven is set at 400° or above, pay attention to whatever it is that you are cooking in the oven. Even carrots can overcook.

*"You do so little to the flounder here, but it ends up so flavorful. Hard to believe it's 'low-fat.'"*

—minutemeals' Chef  Marge

### step 1
## roast the **baby carrots with fresh dill**

1 package (1 pound) baby carrots

1 tablespoon olive oil

1/2 teaspoon salt

2 tablespoons snipped fresh dill

1. Preheat the oven to 425°F.

2. In a small casserole, toss the carrots with the olive oil and salt. Cover tightly and bake for 15 minutes, until tender.

### step 2
## bake the **flounder fillets with mustard, capers, and fennel seed**

4 fresh flounder fillets (1 1/4 pounds total weight)

2 tablespoons country-style Dijon mustard

1/2 teaspoon salt

Freshly ground black pepper to taste

1 tablespoon drained capers

1 teaspoon fennel seeds

1/4 cup dry white wine

1. Rinse the flounder fillets and pat dry. Arrange them in a shallow baking dish large enough to hold them in 1 layer without overlapping. Spread some of the mustard on each fillet and sprinkle the salt, pepper, capers, and fennel seeds over all. Pour the wine around the fillets. Cover the dish with foil and bake for 8 minutes.

2. Remove the foil carefully and bake the fillets another 3 to 4 minutes, just until cooked through.

### step 3
## make the **caramel pudding**

1/3 cup dark brown sugar

1/4 cup cornstarch

1/8 teaspoon salt

2 1/2 cups low-fat (2%) milk

In a medium saucepan, stir together the brown sugar, cornstarch, and salt, crushing any lumps in the brown sugar and cornstarch with the back of the spoon. Gradually stir in the milk until smooth. Place the pan over medium heat and, stirring constantly, bring to a boil. Boil, stirring, until thickened, about 1 minute. Remove from the heat. Pour into 4 serving bowls and chill until serving time, if desired. The pudding can also be served warm.

### step 4
## prepare the **quick slaw**

2 tablespoons rice vinegar

1 teaspoon sugar

1 package (1 pound) pre-shredded cabbage or coleslaw mix

In a serving bowl, stir together the rice vinegar and sugar until the sugar is dissolved. Add the shredded cabbage and toss well to combine. Place on the table.

### step 5
## serve

1. Snip 2 tablespoons fresh dill directly over the carrots, toss, and place the casserole on the table.

2. Place 1 flounder fillet on each of 4 dinner plates. Serve immediately with the slaw as an accompaniment.

3. When ready for dessert, serve the pudding.

---

**Flounder Fillets with Mustard, Capers, and Fennel Seed**
Single serving is 1/4 of the total menu
CALORIES 410; PROTEIN 31g; CARBS 51g; TOTAL FAT 9g; SAT FAT 3g; CHOLESTEROL 79mg; SODIUM 1150mg; FIBER 5g
*19% of calories from fat*

# roasted red snapper
## with olive and tomato sauce

orzo with feta

steamed baby spinach

fresh berries with ladyfingers

## shopping list

Lemon (for juice)

Diced garlic-flavored tomatoes

Chopped green olives with pimientos

Fresh herbs, such as oregano, thyme, rosemary, basil, cilantro, chives, or parsley

Red snapper fillets

Orzo

Feta cheese

Prewashed baby spinach

Ladyfingers (4)

3 cups Fresh seasonal berries (such as blackberries, blue-berries, and raspberries)

Lite Cool Whip

## from your pantry

Onion

Garlic

Olive oil

Sugar

Salt

Freshly ground black pepper

## menu gameplan

serves 4

### beforeyoustart

Preheat the oven to 450°F; bring a saucepan of water to a boil, covered. Rinse the berries and let stand in the colander .

step **1** make the **roasted red snapper with olive and tomato sauce**

step **2** cook the **orzo with feta**

step **3** make the **steamed baby spinach**

step **4** **serve**

## headsup

You'll likely have a few bunches of fresh herbs leftover after making this menu. With some advance planning, you should be able to use them within a few days, when they are at their freshest, in pasta dishes, with sautéed chicken, or in a salad. If you're not likely to use them up right away, substitute dried herbs in the snapper and the orzo, using about half the amounts called for here.

*"All this great food for under 550 calories. It's incredible, shows just how good healthy cooking can be."*

—minutemeals' Chef Miriam

## step 1

### make the **roasted red snapper with olive and tomato sauce**

**for the tomato sauce**

1 onion

2 garlic cloves

1 lemon

1 tablespoon olive oil

1 can (14 ounces) diced garlic-flavored tomatoes

1/4 cup chopped green olives with pimientos

1/2 teaspoon sugar

2 tablespoons chopped fresh herbs, such as oregano, thyme, or rosemary

**for the fish fillets**

4 red snapper fillets (1 1/4 pounds total weight)

1. Preheat the oven to 450°F.

2. Make the tomato sauce: Chop the onion; finely chop the garlic.

3. In a medium nonstick skillet, heat the olive oil over medium-high heat until hot. Add the onion and garlic and cook, stirring, until slightly softened, 2 to 3 minutes. Squeeze 2 tablespoons juice from the lemon.

4. Add the tomatoes, olives, lemon juice, and sugar. Bring the mixture to a simmer and cook, stirring occasionally, for 5 minutes.

5. Chop the fresh herbs to equal 2 tablespoons. Stir the herbs into the tomato sauce right before it comes off the heat.

6. Make the fish fillets: Rinse the snapper fillets and pat dry. Arrange them in a baking dish large enough to hold them in 1 layer without overlapping. Pour the tomato sauce over the fillets, making sure to cover each one. Roast for 8 to 10 minutes. Start checking for doneness around 7 minutes to avoid overcooking. Prod one of the fillets at its thickest point with a fork. It should be opaque, just beginning to flake, and release milky white, not clear or watery, juices. Remove from the oven.

## step 2

### cook the **orzo with feta**

Salt to taste

1 cup orzo

1 teaspoon olive oil

2 tablespoons feta cheese

Freshly ground black pepper to taste

1 tablespoon chopped fresh herbs, such as chives or parsley, or a mix

Fill a 2-quart saucepan with water, salt lightly, and cover. Bring to a boil over high heat. Add the orzo and cook 5 to 7 minutes, or until *al dente*. Drain, transfer to a serving bowl, and toss with the olive oil. Add the feta and freshly ground black pepper and toss again. Keep warm, covered.

## step 3

### steam the **steamed baby spinach**

2 bags (10 ounces each) prewashed baby spinach

1. Put the spinach in a large colander and run under cold water. Do not shake the water off the leaves.

2. Tip the spinach into a large saucepan. Cover and place the pan over high heat. Steam the spinach for 2 minutes, or just until wilted. Remove the pan from the heat.

## step 4

### serve

1. If using fresh herbs with the orzo, add them and toss to combine. Spoon a serving of orzo onto each of 4 dinner plates.

2. Place a snapper fillet on each plate. If using fresh basil, cilantro, or parsley in the sauce with the snapper, stir it in, and spoon the sauce over the fillets and the orzo. Divide the spinach among the plates and serve immediately.

3. When ready for dessert, place a ladyfinger in each dessert bowl and top with 1/2 cup fresh berries and 1 tablespoon of Cool Whip. Serve.

---

**Roasted Red Snapper with Olive and Tomato Sauce Menu**
Single serving is 1/4 of the total menu
CALORIES 527; PROTEIN 42g; CARBS 63g;
TOTAL FAT 12g; SAT FAT 4g; CHOLESTEROL 103mg;
SODIUM 892mg; FIBER 7g

*21% of calories from fat*

# salmon with yogurt-dill sauce

## brown rice with roasted red pepper

## savory zucchini

## almond peaches with angel food cake

**menu gameplan**

### shopping list

Jarred roasted red pepper

Salmon fillets

Lemon (for juice)

Plain fat-free yogurt

Fresh dill

Zucchini

Canned sliced peaches in lite syrup

Angel food cake

Sliced unblanched almonds

### from your pantry

Instant brown rice

Salt and pepper

Olive oil cooking spray

Grainy mustard

Olive oil

Herbes de Provence or fines herbes

Almond extract, optional

serves 4

### beforeyoustart

Add 1 inch water to a large pot, insert a steamer basket, and bring to a boil.

step **1** cook the **brown rice**

step **2** make the **salmon with yogurt-dill sauce**

step **3** cook the **savory zucchini**

step **4** assemble the **almond peaches with angel food cake**

step **5** **serve**

**headsup** In some higher-powered microwave ovens, fish, particularly salmon, may sputter toward the end of cooking time, possibly because the fat in the salmon heats up more quickly than the rest of the fish. If you hear sputtering, check the salmon for doneness; if it needs more time, reduce the power by half for the remainder of cooking time.

*"If you use your microwave for nothing else, use it for fish. Microwaved fillets are perfectly moist every time."* —minutemeals' Chef Ruth

## cook the **brown rice with roasted pepper**

1 3/4 cups water

2 cups instant brown rice

3 tablespoons chopped roasted red pepper

Bring the water to a boil in a medium saucepan, covered, over high heat. Stir in the rice and salt. Return to a boil, reduce the heat to low, cover, and cook for 5 minutes. Remove the pan from the heat and stir in the roasted pepper. Cover and let stand until serving time.

## step 2

## make the **salmon with yogurt-dill sauce**

### for the fish

Olive oil cooking spray

4 salmon fillets from the tail end (each about 5 ounces), skin removed

1 lemon (for juice)

Salt and pepper to taste

### for the sauce

1 container (8 ounces) plain fat-free yogurt

2 tablespoons snipped fresh dill

2 tablespoons grainy mustard

1. Cook the fish: Select a shallow microwave-safe casserole or rectangular dish large enough to hold the salmon in a single layer. Spray the dish with olive oil spray. Arrange the salmon skinned-side down in the prepared dish. Squeeze 1 tablespoon juice from the lemon and sprinkle over the salmon. Season with salt and pepper.

2. Cover the dish tightly with microwave-safe plastic wrap. Microwave on High for 4 to 5 minutes, rotating the dish halfway through the cooking time, until the fish is just opaque in the center but still moist.

3. While the fish cooks, make the sauce: Place the yogurt in a small bowl. Snip enough dill to measure 2 tablespoons. Stir the mustard and chopped dill into the yogurt; season with black pepper.

## step 3

## cook the **savory zucchini**

4 small or 3 medium zucchini

2 teaspoons olive oil

2 teaspoons herbes de Provence or fines herbes

1. Add 1 inch water to a large pot, insert a steamer basket, cover, and bring to a boil over high heat. Trim the ends of the zucchini and cut each in half lengthwise. Cut crosswise into 1/2-inch slices. Place the zucchini in the steamer basket, cover, reduce the heat to medium, and steam the zucchini until just tender, about 8 minutes.

2. Place the steamed zucchini in a serving bowl. Drizzle with the olive oil and sprinkle with the herbs and salt and pepper. Cover to keep warm.

## step 4

## assemble the **almond peaches with angel food cake**

1 can (about 15 1/4 ounces) sliced peaches in lite syrup

1/8 teaspoon almond extract, optional

4 thin slices angel food cake

2 tablespoons sliced unblanched almonds

Place the peaches in a small bowl. Stir in the almond extract, if using, and chill until serving time. Place the angel food cake slices on dessert plates and cover with a dish towel.

## step 5

## serve

1. Place a salmon fillet on each of 4 dinner plates. Drizzle some of the yogurt sauce over each serving.

2. Fluff the rice with a fork and season with pepper. Spoon servings of rice and zucchini next to the salmon fillets.

3. When ready for dessert, spoon the peaches over the angel food cake, adding syrup to moisten the cake and the fruit. Sprinkle each serving with almonds and serve.

**Salmon with Yogurt-Dill Sauce**
Single serving is 1/4 of the total menu

CALORIES 544; PROTEIN 38g; CARBS 74g; TOTAL FAT 10g; SAT FAT 1g; CHOLESTEROL 73mg; SODIUM 993mg; FIBER 6g

*17% of calories from fat*

# salmon with gremolita
### shredded potatoes
### cucumber salad
### strawberries with sweet balsamic

## shopping list

Refrigerated shredded hash brown potatoes

Tomato

Hothouse cucumber

Shallot

Reduced-fat feta cheese

Cilantro

Lime (for juice)

Salmon fillets

Strawberries

## from your pantry

Olive oil cooking spray

Salt

Freshly ground black pepper

Garlic

Brown sugar

Balsamic vinegar

**headsup** Gremolita is an Italian garnish of chopped parsley, lemon zest, and garlic. It is generally sprinkled on or stirred into a dish at the end of the cooking time. The Italian combination would work here, too; if you like, simply sprinkle either mixture over the broiled salmon as soon as it comes out of the oven.

**menu gameplan**

serves 4

**before**you**start**

Preheat the broiler.

step 1 cook the **shredded potatoes**

step 2 make the **cucumber salad**

step 3 make the **salmon with gremolita**

step 4 assemble the **strawberries with sweet balsamic**

step 5 **serve**

*"Salmon is a rich fish. Herbs and citrus give it the fresh, clean note I want."*

—minutemeals' Chef  Wendy

## cook the **shredded potatoes**

> Olive oil cooking spray
>
> 2 cups refrigerated shredded hash brown potatoes
>
> Salt and freshly ground black pepper to taste

Coat a nonstick 12-inch skillet with olive oil spray. Heat the skillet over moderately high heat. Spread the potatoes evenly in the pan. Season with salt and pepper. Cook, stirring occasionally 12 minutes, until tender and browned.

### step 2

## make the **cucumber salad**

> 1 medium tomato
>
> 1 hothouse cucumber
>
> 1 shallot
>
> 1/3 cup reduced-fat feta cheese
>
> Salt and freshly ground black pepper

**1.** Coarsely chop the tomato. Thinly slice the cucumber. Chop the shallot.

**2.** In a salad bowl mix the cucumber, shallot, feta cheese, and tomato. Season with salt and pepper. Place the salad bowl on the table.

### step 3

## make the **salmon with gremolita**

> Olive oil cooking spray
>
> 1/2 cup chopped cilantro
>
> 2 small cloves garlic, chopped
>
> 1 tablespoon lime juice
>
> 1 1/2 teaspoons chopped garlic
>
> 4 salmon fillets, each 6 ounces
>
> Salt and freshly ground black pepper to taste

**1.** Preheat the broiler. Line a broiler pan with aluminum foil. Spray the broiler-pan rack with olive oil cooking spray.

**2.** Chop the cilantro and garlic. Squeeze 1 tablespoon of juice from the lime. In a small bowl combine the cilantro, garlic, and lime juice.

**3.** Season the salmon with salt and pepper. Place the fillets on the prepared broiler pan and coat with the cilantro mixture. Broil the salmon 5 inches from the heat for 6 to 8 minutes, or until opaque in the thickest part.

### step 4

## assemble the **strawberries with sweet balsamic**

> 2 cups strawberries
>
> 2 teaspoons brown sugar
>
> 1 teaspoon balsamic vinegar

Rinse and hull the strawberries. Halve and place in a serving bowl. Sprinkle the brown sugar and balsamic vinegar over and stir gently.

### step 5

## serve

**1.** Transfer a salmon fillet to each of 4 dinner plates. Place a serving of shredded potatoes on each plate, and place the plates on the table. Serve with the salad.

**2.** When ready for dessert, divide the strawberries among 4 dessert dishes and serve.

---

**Salmon with Gremolita**
Single serving is 1/4 of the total menu

CALORIES 369; PROTEIN 41g; CARBS 31g;
TOTAL FAT 9g; SAT FAT 3g; CHOLESTEROL 92mg;
SODIUM 835mg; FIBER 4g

*23% of calories from fat*

# salmon and potato patties

### lemon-tarragon carrots
### greens with honey-mustard dressing
### tangerines

## menu gameplan

serves 4

## **before**youstart

Bring a medium saucepan of water to a boil, covered, over high heat, to cook the carrots.

step **1** cook the **salmon and potato patties**

step **2** while the fish cakes cook, make the **lemon-tarragon carrots**

step **3** prepare the **greens with honey-mustard dressing**

step **4** **serve**

## shopping list

Scallion

Cilantro or parsley

Eggs

Canned skinless boneless salmon

Prepared mashed potatoes

Frozen corn kernels

Baby carrots

Lemon

Prewashed baby greens mix

Grape tomatoes

Tangerines

## from your pantry

Mild Louisiana-style cayenne pepper sauce

Vegetable oil

Butter

Dried tarragon

Salt and pepper

Orange juice

Honey mustard

Extra virgin olive oil

## lucky**for**you
Canned salmon is now available without the soft, edible bones that children, in particular, just don't like. However, if you don't mind the bones, using the bone-in canned salmon here will add 135 or more milligrams of calcium to each serving—more calcium than you'll get from 1/2 cup of cottage cheese.

*"Salmon patties were a childhood staple. Even updated with cilantro and corn, they make me feel like a kid."*

—minutemeals' Chef Paul

## step 1

### cook the **salmon and potato patties**

- 1 scallion
- 1/4 cup loosely packed cilantro or parsley leaves
- 2 large eggs
- 2 tablespoons mild Louisiana-style cayenne pepper sauce
- 2 cans (6 ounces each) skinless boneless salmon, drained
- 1 cup prepared mashed potatoes made without fat
- 1/2 cup frozen corn kernels
- 1 teaspoon vegetable oil

1. Finely chop the scallion and cilantro or parsley; place in a medium bowl. Add the eggs and pepper sauce; beat with a fork to blend. Drain the salmon well and flake it. Add the salmon, mashed potatoes, and corn to the egg mixture and stir to mix.

2. Place 1/2 teaspoon of the oil in a large nonstick skillet over medium heat. Spoon the salmon mixture into the skillet, making 4 even mounds; flatten each into 4-inch-diameter cakes. Cover and cook for 10 minutes, turning once and adding the remaining 1/2 teaspoon oil if necessary, until the salmon patties are hot throughout and golden brown.

## step 2

### while the fish cakes cook, make the **lemon-tarragon carrots**

- 1 pound baby carrots
- 1 lemon
- 1/2 teaspoon butter
- 1/4 teaspoon dried tarragon
- 1/8 teaspoon salt
- Pepper to taste

1. Bring a medium saucepan of water to a boil, covered, over high heat. Add the carrots, cover, reduce the heat to medium, and simmer the carrots for 8 to 10 minutes until tender. While the carrots are cooking, grate 1 teaspoon of zest from the lemon. (Save the lemon for serving the salmon patties.)

2. Drain the carrots and return them to the saucepan. Add the butter, lemon zest, tarragon, salt, and pepper and toss over low heat for 1 minute, until the butter is melted.

## step 3

### prepare the **greens with honey-mustard dressing**

- 1 bag (5 ounces) mixed baby greens
- 1 cup grape tomatoes
- 2 tablespoons orange juice
- 2 tablespoons honey mustard
- 2 teaspoons extra virgin olive oil

Place the lettuce and tomatoes in a large salad bowl. Shake together the orange juice, mustard, and olive oil in a small jar with a lid until blended. Pour the dressing over the salad, season with salt and pepper, and toss. Place the salad on the table.

## step 4

### serve

1. Cut the reserved lemon into wedges. Place a salmon patty and a lemon wedge on each of 4 dinner plates. Spoon a serving of carrots on each plate and bring to the table. Serve with the salad.

2. When ready for dessert, serve 1 tangerine per person on 4 dessert plates.

---

**Salmon and Potato Patties**
Single serving is 1/4 of the total menu
CALORIES 357; PROTEIN 26g; CARBS 41g;
TOTAL FAT 12g; SAT FAT 2g; CHOLESTEROL 159mg;
SODIUM 580mg; FIBER 6g
*30% of calories from fat*

# orange-soy glazed salmon

parslied new potatoes

baby peas with carrots and ginger

ripe pears and plums with almond cookies

## shopping list

Small red potatoes

Flat-leaf parsley

Salmon fillet

Frozen baby peas

Shredded carrots
(from the produce department
or salad bar)

Fresh gingerroot

Ripe pears or plums

Almond crescent cookies

## from your pantry

Red wine vinegar

Extra virgin olive oil

Salt

Freshly ground black pepper

Cooking spray

Orange juice

Lite soy sauce

Ground ginger

Garlic powder

Cornstarch

Butter

serves 4

## **before**youstart

Preheat the oven to 450°F to roast the salmon. Bring the water to a boil in a medium saucepan, covered.

step 1 make the **parslied new potatoes**

step 2 make the **orange-soy glazed salmon**

step 3 make the **baby peas with carrots and ginger**

step 4 serve

## **heads**up

A "slurry"—cornstarch dissolved in a tiny amount of water—makes it possible to achieve a lump-free glaze. If dry cornstarch is added directly to the hot orange-soy mixture, it will clump as soon as it hits the liquid.

*"The orange-soy glaze is delicious on chicken and steak, too, and the ingredients are probably right in your pantry."*

—minutemeals' Chef Sarah

## step 1
### make the **parslied new potatoes**

1¹/2 pounds small red potatoes, 1 to 1¹/2 inches in diameter, halved or quartered if larger

2 tablespoons chopped fresh flat-leaf parsley

1 tablespoon red wine vinegar

2 teaspoons extra virgin olive oil

¹/4 teaspoon salt

¹/8 teaspoon freshly ground pepper

1. Bring a large pot of water to a boil, covered, over high heat. Halve or quarter the larger potatoes.

2. Add the potatoes to the boiling water, cover, and simmer 12 to 15 minutes, or until the potatoes are tender when pierced with the tip of a sharp knife.

3. Meanwhile, chop enough parsley to measure 2 tablespoons. Drain the potatoes and return to the saucepan. Add the parsley, vinegar, oil, salt, and pepper. Gently toss to combine.

## step 2
### make the **orange-soy glazed salmon**

Cooking spray

1 salmon fillet, about 1¹/4 pounds

¹/4 cup orange juice

1 tablespoon lite soy sauce

¹/4 teaspoon ground ginger

¹/4 teaspoon garlic powder

³/4 teaspoon cornstarch, dissolved in 1 teaspoon water

1. Preheat the oven to 450°F. Coat a shallow baking dish with non-stick cooking spray. Place the salmon fillet in the prepared dish.

2. Combine the orange juice, soy sauce, ginger, and garlic powder in a small saucepan. Bring to a boil; reduce the heat and simmer for 4 minutes.

3. Stir the cornstarch mixture into the saucepan and simmer, stirring, until thickened and glossy, about 30 seconds.

4. Spread 1 tablespoon of the sauce over the salmon fillet. Bake for 5 minutes. Spread with the remaining sauce and bake 5 minutes longer, or until the fish is just opaque in the thickest part.

## step 3
### cook the **baby peas with carrots and ginger**

1 box (10 ounces) frozen baby peas

³/4 cup shredded carrots

¹/2 cup water

¹/2 teaspoon grated ginger

¹/2 teaspoon butter

¹/8 teaspoon salt

1. Combine the peas, carrot, and water in a skillet. Bring to a boil, reduce the heat, and simmer 4 to 5 minutes, or until the peas are tender.

2. Finely grate ¹/2 teaspoon ginger. Drain any water from the peas and stir in the ginger, butter, and salt.

## step 4
### serve

1. Cut the salmon into 4 pieces and divide among 4 dinner plates. Add servings of potatoes and peas to each plate, and bring to the table.

2. When ready for dessert, arrange the fruit in a bowl. Place 2 almond crescent cookies on each of 4 dessert plates and serve with the fruit.

**Orange-Soy Glazed Salmon**
Single serving is ¹/4 of the total menu, with 1 pear per serving

CALORIES 546; PROTEIN 38g; CARBS 79g; TOTAL FAT 10g; SAT FAT 2g; CHOLESTEROL 75mg; SODIUM 629mg; FIBER 12g

*16% of calories from fat*

# garlic-lime swordfish
## with oven-grilled vegetables
### roasted-garlic couscous
### micro-steamed cauliflower
### orange-topped pound cake

## menu gameplan

**shopping list**

Swordfish

Limes (for zest and juice)

Cherry tomatoes
(from the salad bar)

Scallions

Precut cauliflower florets

Roasted-garlic and olive oil couscous

Reduced-fat pound cake

Orange marmalade

Vanilla fat-free yogurt

**from your pantry**

Olive oil cooking spray

Tomato paste

Sugar

Salt

Freshly ground black pepper

Fat-free reduced-sodium chicken broth

Orange juice

Olive oil

serves 4

**before**youstart

Preheat the broiler.

step 1 make the **garlic-lime swordfish with oven-grilled vegetables**

step 2 make the **micro-steamed cauliflower**

step 3 make the **roasted garlic couscous**

step 4 prepare the **orange-topped pound cake**

step 5 **serve**

**heads**up Tomato paste comes in squeeze tubes—no more throwing out half-empty cans. If you can't find a tube, though, freeze leftovers from a can in tablespoon-size scoops, then transfer them to self-sealing plastic freezer bags.

*"Swordfish is really meaty, perfect for kabobs. To save time, I didn't skewer it; you can if you're planning to grill."*

—minutemeals' Chef Marge

## make the **lime-garlic swordfish with oven-grilled vegetables**

Olive oil cooking spray

1 pound swordfish

2 to 3 limes

1 tablespoon tomato paste

1/2 teaspoon sugar

Salt and freshly ground black pepper to taste

1 cup cherry tomatoes

2 bunches scallions

1. Preheat the broiler. Coat 2 jelly-roll pans with olive oil spray. Cut the swordfish into 1-inch chunks and place on 1 of the prepared pans.

2. Grate 1 teaspoon of lime zest into a small bowl. Squeeze 2 tablespoons of juice from the limes and add to the zest. Stir in the tomato paste, sugar, and salt and pepper. Pour over the swordfish and toss to coat.

3. Rinse and stem the cherry tomatoes. Trim the scallions. Cut off all but 4 inches of the green tops. Place the cherry tomatoes and scallions on the other prepared jelly-roll pan. Coat with olive oil spray and season with salt and pepper.

4. Broil the tomatoes and scallions 5 inches from the heat until lightly charred. Transfer to a serving platter and cover loosely with foil.

5. Broil the swordfish for 4 to 6 minutes, without turning, until just opaque in the thickest part. Transfer fish and juices to the platter with the vegetables. Leave the broiler on for the pound cake, Step 4.

## step 2

## make the **micro-steamed cauliflower**

1 bag (12 ounces) cut cauliflower florets

Place the cauliflower in a microwave-safe dish. Sprinkle with water. Cover with a lid or vented plastic wrap. Microwave on High 6 to 7 minutes, or until tender. Drain and season with salt and pepper. Cover loosely to keep warm.

## step 3

## make the **roasted-garlic couscous**

3/4 cup fat-free reduced-sodium chicken broth

1/2 cup orange juice

1 teaspoon olive oil

1 package (5.8 ounces) roasted garlic and olive oil couscous

1. In a medium saucepan bring the broth, orange juice, olive oil, and the couscous seasoning packet to a boil, covered, over high heat.

2. Stir in the couscous and remove from the heat. Cover and let stand while you prepare the pound cake.

## step 4

## prepare the **orange-topped pound cake**

4 slices reduced-fat pound cake

2 tablespoons orange marmalade

1 container (8 ounces) vanilla fat-free yogurt

Arrange the pound cake slices on a small cookie sheet. Spread one side of each piece of pound cake with the marmalade. Broil 5 inches from the heat for 2 minutes, or until the marmalade is bubbly and the cake is toasted.

## step 5

## serve

1. Bring the cauliflower to the table.

2. Fluff the couscous and place on a large serving platter. Arrange the broiled fish and vegetables on top, leaving a border of couscous around the edge of the platter. Place the platter on the table and serve.

3. When ready for dessert, transfer the pound cake slices to 4 dessert dishes. Top each with vanilla yogurt, dividing evenly, and serve.

---

**Garlic-Lime Swordfish**
Single serving is 1/4 of the total menu
CALORIES 687; PROTEIN 32g; CARBS 99g;
TOTAL FAT 20g; SAT FAT 8g; CHOLESTEROL 141mg;
SODIUM 1049mg; FIBER 6g

*25% of calories from fat*

# citrus-herb fish packets

## couscous with toasted pine nuts
## cherry tomato salad
## blackberry and lemon yogurt parfaits

### shopping list

Fresh blackberries

Lemon fat-free yogurt

Sugar snap peas

Tilapia fillets

Lemon (for zest and juice)

Fresh dill

Couscous mix with toasted pine nuts

Crumbled feta cheese

Pitted kalamata olives

Basil leaves

Capers

### from the salad bar

Red pepper slices

Red onion slices

Cherry tomatoes

### from your pantry

Sugar

Salt

Freshly ground black pepper

Garlic

Fruity olive oil

Balsamic vinegar

serves 4

## beforeyoustart

Preheat the oven to 450°F to cook the fish.

| step | 1 | make the **blackberry and lemon yogurt parfaits** |
| step | 2 | cook the **citrus-herb fish packets** |
| step | 3 | cook the **couscous with toasted pine nuts** |
| step | 4 | assemble the **cherry tomato salad** |
| step | 5 | serve |

luckyforyou You can use either a lime or an orange to make the vinaigrette instead of a lemon. If you do use an orange, increase the juice to 2 tablespoons; oranges are less acidic than lemon and lime so you can boost the flavor without worrying about overdoing the acidity. Don't up the amount of zest, however; the teaspoon called for is plenty flavorful.

*"An incredible aroma fills the room when the fish packets are opened—such a lovely way to start a meal."*

—minutemeals' Chef Sarah

### step 1

## make the **blackberry and lemon yogurt parfaits**

2 cups fresh blackberries

1 teaspoon sugar

2 containers (8 ounces each) lemon fat-free yogurt

1. In a medium bowl, toss the blackberries with the sugar.

2. Place about 1/4 cup blackberries in the bottom of each of 4 wine glasses; reserve the remaining berries for serving. Top each with 1/2 cup lemon yogurt. Refrigerate the parfaits.

### step 2

## cook the **citrus-herb fish packets**

2 cups red pepper slices, halved

1/2 cup red onion slices, chopped

1 cup sugar snap peas

4 tilapia fillets, 5 ounces each

1/2 teaspoon salt

1/4 teaspoon freshly ground black pepper

1 lemon

1 tablespoon chopped dill

1 small garlic clove

1 tablespoon fruity olive oil

1. Preheat the oven to 450°F. Tear off four 18- × 12-inch lengths of heavy duty aluminum foil. Lay the foil pieces on a work surface, with the short sides towards you.

2. Cut the red pepper slices in half. Chop the red onion slices. Arrange the peppers, onions, and sugar snap peas in the center of the front half of each piece of foil, dividing evenly. Top each mound with a tilapia fillet. Season all 4 fillets, using 1/4 teaspoon of the salt and 1/8 teaspoon of pepper.

3. Fold the foil over the fish so the edges meet and seal the edge by rolling it over tightly. Place the packets on a baking sheet. Bake the fish 10 minutes.

4. While the fish bakes, prepare the vinaigrette: Wash and dry the lemon. Finely grate 1 teaspoon zest. Squeeze 1 tablespoon juice. Chop 1 tablespoon dill. In a small bowl, combine the remaining 1/4 teaspoon salt and 1/8 teaspoon pepper, the lemon zest, lemon juice, and dill. Crush the garlic into the bowl with a garlic press and add the oil; whisk until blended.

### step 3

## cook the **couscous with toasted pine nuts**

1 1/4 cups water

1 box (5.6 ounces) couscous mix with toasted pine nuts

Prepare the couscous according to the package directions.

### step 4

## assemble the **cherry tomato salad**

1 pint cherry tomatoes, halved

1 tablespoon balsamic vinegar

Freshly ground pepper to taste

2 tablespoons crumbled feta cheese

6 pitted kalamata olives, chopped

4 large basil leaves, chopped

1 teaspoon capers

1. Halve the cherry tomatoes. Place on a serving platter. Drizzle with the vinegar and season with pepper. Sprinkle with the feta cheese.

2. Chop the olives and basil. Sprinkle the tomatoes with the olives, basil, and capers.

### step 5

## serve

1. Fluff the couscous with a fork.

2. Pierce the fish packets to release the steam and peel back the foil. Transfer vegetables and fish to dinner plates. Stir the vinaigrette and spoon it over the fish. Serve with the couscous and tomato salad.

3. For dessert, divide reserved berries among the parfaits; serve.

---

**Citrus-Herb Fish Packets**
**Single serving is 1/4 of total menu**
CALORIES 246; PROTEIN 27g; CARBS 15g;
TOTAL FAT 9g; SAT FAT 2g; CHOLESTEROL 63mg;
SODIUM 525mg; FIBER 3g
*17% of calories from fat*

# middle eastern spiced tuna steaks

## garlic couscous
## mixed sautéed vegetables
## ripe plums and pears

**menu gameplan**

### shopping list

Garlic-flavored chicken broth

Couscous

Fresh flat-leaf parsley

Chopped or slivered
sun-dried tomatoes in oil

Tuna steaks

Zucchini

Yellow pepper slices
(from the salad bar)

Matchstick-cut carrots (from
the produce department)

Ripe plums

Pears

### from your pantry

Olive oil cooking spray

Dried mint

Ground cumin

Ground cinnamon

Salt

Ground ginger or nutmeg

Cayenne pepper

Garlic

Olive oil

serves 4

## beforeyoustart

Bring the broth to a boil in a medium
saucepan, covered. Preheat the broiler
to cook the tuna.

step 1 cook the **garlic couscous**

step 2 cook the **middle eastern spiced tuna steaks**

step 3 cook the **mixed sautéed vegetables**

step 4 **serve**

## headsup
Tuna is a lean fish and, like
lean meat, is best cooked to
rare, or medium-rare at most. Cooked any more than that,
it will be dry and tough.

*"If time permits, slice the tuna and fan the slices next to the vegetables. The rainbow of colors is really striking."*

—minutemeals' Chef Marge

## step 1

### cook the **garlic couscous**

1 can (14 ounces) garlic-flavored chicken broth

1 cup couscous

2 tablespoons chopped fresh flat-leaf parsley

1 tablespoon chopped or slivered sun-dried tomatoes in oil, blotted dry

**1.** Bring the broth to a boil in a medium saucepan, covered, over high heat. Stir in the couscous. Cover and remove from the heat.

**2.** Meanwhile, chop enough parsley to measure 2 tablespoons. Chop any large pieces of sun-dried tomato.

**3.** Stir the parsley and sun-dried tomatoes into the couscous and fluff with a fork.

## step 2

### cook the **middle eastern spiced tuna steaks**

Olive oil cooking spray

1 tablespoon dried mint

1 teaspoon ground cumin

1/2 teaspoon ground cinnamon

1/2 teaspoon salt

1/4 teaspoon ground ginger or nutmeg

1/8 teaspoon cayenne pepper

4 tuna steaks each 3/4 to 1-inch thick (1 1/2 pounds total)

**1.** Preheat the boiler. Line the broiler pan with aluminum foil. Spray the broiler-pan rack with olive oil spray.

**2.** In a small bowl stir together the mint, cumin, cinnamon, salt, ginger or nutmeg, and cayenne pepper in a small bowl.

**3.** Sprinkle the spice mixture on both sides of the tuna steaks, patting the spice mixture so it adheres. Spray both sides of the tuna steaks with olive oil spray. Place the tuna steaks on the prepared broiler-pan rack.

**4.** Broil the tuna 4 inches from the heat for 4 to 8 minutes, turning once, or until cooked to desired degree of doneness.

## step 3

### cook the **mixed sautéed vegetables**

1 medium zucchini, diced

1 cup yellow pepper slices, diced

1 large garlic clove

2 teaspoons olive oil

1 cup matchstick-cut carrots

1/8 teaspoon salt

**1.** Dice the zucchini and yellow pepper. Smash the garlic with the flat side of a chef's knife.

**2.** Heat the olive oil in a large non-stick skillet over medium heat. Add the smashed garlic clove. Heat until the garlic is golden.

**3.** Add the zucchini, pepper, carrots, and salt to the skillet. Cook, stirring, for 2 to 3 minutes, or until the vegetables are crisp-tender. (If the vegetables appear to be dry, add a tablespoon of broth or water as they cook.) Remove and discard the garlic. Transfer the vegetables to a serving dish and place on the table.

## step 4

### serve

**1.** Transfer 1 tuna steak to each of 4 dinner plates.

**2.** Fluff the couscous again with a fork and place in a serving dish; place on the table. Serve the couscous and vegetables with the tuna steaks.

**3.** When ready for dessert, serve the plums and pears.

---

**Middle Eastern Spiced Tuna Steaks**
Single serving is (1/4) of the total menu
CALORIES 492; PROTEIN 47g; CARBS 64g;
TOTAL FAT 5g; SAT FAT 1g; CHOLESTEROL 74mg;
SODIUM 855mg; FIBER 8g
*10% of calories from fat*

# deli-style tuna salad over greens

sliced tomatoes

seeded crisp breads

balsamic-flavored ice cream with strawberries

## shopping list

Arugula

Canned white tuna packed in water

Scallions

Celery

Pimiento-stuffed green olives

Lemons (for juice)

Shredded carrots (from the salad bar or the produce department)

Strawberries

Vanilla low-fat ice cream

Ripe tomatoes

Seeded crisp bread

## from your pantry

Extra virgin olive oil

Freshly ground black pepper

Sugar

Balsamic vinegar

Salt

serves 4

## **before**youstart

Take the ice cream out of the freezer to soften slightly.

step **1** make the **deli-style tuna salad over greens**

step **2** assemble the **balsamic-flavored ice cream with strawberries**

step **3** slice the **tomatoes**

step **4** **serve**

luckyforyou To soften ice cream or frozen yogurt in an instant, just microwave it Medium-High for 20 to 30 seconds. To make the dessert here even easier, simply mix the balsamic vinegar with the strawberries and spoon the mixture over the ice cream.

*"I stock up on canned tuna in the summer, and serve this meal when it's almost too hot to eat."*

—minutemeals' Chef Miriam

step 1

## make the **deli-style tuna salad over greens**

1 large bunch arugula

2 cans (6 ounces each) white tuna in water

3 scallions, thinly sliced

2 celery stalks, thinly sliced

1/4 cup pimiento-stuffed green olives

1 to 2 lemons

1/2 cup shredded carrots

2 tablespoons extra virgin olive oil

1/4 teaspoon freshly ground black pepper

**1.** Trim any tough stems from the arugula. Wash and spin dry. Spread the arugula on a serving platter.

**2.** Drain both cans of tuna, transfer to a medium bowl, and flake with a fork. Thinly slice the scallions and the celery. Coarsely chop the olives. Squeeze 2 tablespoons of juice from the lemon(s).

**3.** Add the shredded carrots, olive oil, black pepper, celery, scallions, olives, and lemon juice to the tuna and toss to mix well. Mound the tuna salad on top of the arugula.

step 2

## assemble the **balsamic-flavored ice cream with strawberries**

1 pint fresh strawberries

1 teaspoon sugar

1 pint vanilla low-fat ice cream

1 tablespoon balsamic vinegar

**1.** Rinse the strawberries, cut off their green tops, and slice them into chunks into a small bowl. Sprinkle with sugar and let stand until ready to serve.

**2.** Scoop the softened ice cream into a medium mixing bowl. Stir in the balsamic vinegar. Place in the freezer until ready to serve.

step 3

## slice the **tomatoes**

2 large ripe tomatoes

Salt and pepper to taste

Slice the tomatoes and arrange on a plate. Season with salt and pepper.

step 4

## serve

**1.** Place 16 seeded crisp breads (4 per person) in a basket and place on the table. Pass the platter of tuna salad and the plate of tomatoes and let diners help themselves.

**2.** When ready for dessert, scoop 1/2 cup of ice cream into each of 4 small bowls. Divide the strawberries and their juice among the bowls. Serve immediately.

---

**Deli-Style Tuna Salad Over Greens**
Single serving is 1/4 of the total menu
CALORIES 455; PROTEIN 29g; CARBS 53g;
TOTAL FAT 15g; SAT FAT 3g; CHOLESTEROL 41mg;
SODIUM 1048mg; FIBER 7g

*29% of calories from fat*

# mussels in spicy sauce

grilled country garlic bread

spring greens salad with creamy Italian dressing

minted fruit salad

menu gameplan

serves 4

step 1 make the **mussels in spicy sauce**

step 2 make the **grilled country garlic bread**

step 3 make the **salad**

step 4 **serve**

## shopping list

Mussels, farm-raised if available

Shallot

Five-spice powder

Clam juice

Country-style bread

Pre-washed spring greens mix

Grape tomatoes

Low-fat creamy Italian salad dressing

Fresh fruit salad (1 pound, from the salad bar or produce department)

Fresh mint

## from your pantry

Olive oil

Tomato paste

Red pepper flakes

White wine

Garlic

Pepper

## luckyforyou

Farm-raised mussels are widely available and, unlike their wild counterparts, are almost completely free of grit, mud, and even the beard that must be removed before cooking, making cleaning far less time-consuming than it used to be. And, the meat in cultivated mussels tends to be larger than in wild mussels, a nice bonus.

*"It's hard to be formal when you're shelling and dipping mussels. Serve them when you want a fun, casual meal."* —minutemeals' Chef Wendy

### step 1

## make the **mussels in spicy sauce**

- 2 pounds mussels
- 1 shallot, chopped
- 1 1/2 teaspoons olive oil
- 1 teaspoon tomato paste
- 3/4 teaspoon five-spice powder
- 3/4 teaspoon crushed red pepper flakes
- 4 ounces clam juice
- 4 ounces white wine

1. Scrub the mussels and remove any beards under cold running water. Chop the shallot.

2. Heat the oil in a large deep skillet or Dutch oven over medium heat. Add the shallot and cook, stirring, for 1 minute or until it begins to soften. Add the tomato paste, five-spice powder, and crushed red pepper, and cook, stirring constantly, for about 1 minute.

3. Stir in the clam juice and the white wine. Add the mussels. Cover and steam about 5 minutes, shaking the pan occasionally, until the mussels open. Transfer the mussels to a serving bowl with a slotted spoon. Discard any mussels that do not open. Strain the cooking liquid into a small serving bowl.

### step 2

## make the **grilled country garlic bread**

- 4 slices (each 1 ounce) country-style bread
- 1 garlic clove

1. Cut the bread into 4 thick slices. Cut the garlic clove in half lengthwise.

2. In a toaster or toaster oven, toast the bread until just crisp and golden brown on both sides. Rub the cut sides of the garlic clove over one side of each piece of toast. Place the bread in a basket and bring to the table.

### step 3

## make the **spring greens salad with creamy italian dressing**

- 1 package (5 ounces) spring greens mix
- 2 cups grape tomatoes
- 2 tablespoons low-fat creamy Italian salad dressing
- Pepper to taste

In a salad bowl, place the greens mix, grape tomatoes, salad dressing, and pepper. Toss to mix and place on the table with 4 salad plates.

### step 4

## serve

1. Divide the mussels among 4 serving bowls. Place the strained cooking liquid on the table, and let diners remove the mussel meat from the shell and dip in the sauce. Pass the toasts and the salad.

2. When ready for dessert, place the fruit salad in a serving bowl. Snip enough mint to measure 2 tablespoons, and toss with the fruit salad. Serve.

---

**Mussels in Spicy Sauce**
Single serving is 1/4 of the total menu
CALORIES 416; PROTEIN 32g; CARBS 51g; TOTAL FAT 9g; SAT FAT 2g; CHOLESTEROL 64mg; SODIUM 1116mg; FIBER 5g

*20% of calories from fat*

# scallops and asian vegetables
## gingered garlic rice
## caramel-drizzled pineapple

## shopping list

Fresh gingerroot

Roasted garlic in purée

Napa cabbage

Scallions

Sea scallops

Frozen Oriental mixed vegetables

Peeled and cored fresh pineapple, from the produce department

Fat-free caramel sauce

## from your pantry

Instant brown rice

Salt

Canola oil

Toasted sesame oil

Rice vinegar

Lite soy sauce

Honey

Rum or rum extract

serves 4

### beforeyoustart

Bring the water to a boil in a medium saucepan, covered, over high heat to cook the rice.

step 1 cook the **gingered garlic rice**

step 2 stir-fry the **scallops and asian vegetables**

step 3 assemble the **caramel-drizzled pineapple**

step 4 **serve**

## headsup

The scallops will brown better if you pat them dry with paper towels before searing. The same is true for meat, poultry, and fish.

*"Scallops go from cooked to overcooked in under a minute. The 4-minute cooking time here is really all they need."*

—minutemeals' Chef Paul

## step 1

### cook the **gingered garlic rice**

2 cups instant brown rice

2 teaspoons grated fresh ginger

1 1/2 teaspoons roasted garlic in purée

1/4 teaspoon salt

Prepare the rice according to package directions, adding the ginger and garlic with the rice, and reducing the salt to 1/4 teaspoon.

## step 2

### stir-fry the **scallops and asian vegetables**

2 cups sliced napa cabbage

4 scallions

1/2-inch piece of fresh ginger

2 teaspoons canola oil

1 pound sea scallops, rinsed and patted dry

1 1/2 teaspoons toasted sesame oil

3 cups (12 ounces) frozen Oriental mixed vegetables

2 tablespoons rice vinegar

2 tablespoons lite soy sauce

2 teaspoons honey

**1.** Thinly slice the cabbage and scallions. Cut the ginger into thin slices; stack the slices and cut into small matchsticks

**2.** Heat the canola oil in a large non-stick skillet over medium-high heat. Add the scallops and cook for 3 minutes, turning once, until almost opaque in the center. Transfer to a plate. Add the sesame oil, cabbage, scallions, and ginger to the skillet. Stir-fry 1 minute. Add the frozen vegetables and stir-fry 4 minutes more, or until the vegetables are crisp-tender.

**3.** Add the vinegar, soy sauce, and honey, tossing to coat the vegetables. Add the scallops and cook, stirring gently, 1 minute more.

## step 3

### assemble the **caramel-drizzled pineapple**

1 peeled and cored fresh pineapple

1/3 cup fat-free caramel sauce

2 teaspoons rum or 1/8 teaspoon rum extract

Slice the pineapple into rings and divide among 4 dessert dishes. Chill until ready to serve. Place the caramel sauce and rum or rum extract in a small microwave-safe dish.

## step 4

### serve

**1.** Divide the rice among 4 shallow bowls, and top with the scallop and vegetable stir-fry.

**2.** When ready for dessert, microwave the caramel mixture on High for 40 seconds. Stir well to blend. Drizzle over pineapple and serve.

---

**Scallops and Asian Vegetables**
Single serving is 1/4 of the total menu
CALORIES 438; PROTEIN 18g; CARBS 78g;
TOTAL FAT 8g; SAT FAT 1g; CHOLESTEROL 18mg;
SODIUM 645mg; FIBER 7g

*15% of calories from fat*

# pan-seared sea scallops

couscous with herbs

spinach, radicchio, and orange salad

warm sliced peaches with peach sorbet

## menu gameplan

serves 4

|  | | |
|---|---|---|
| step | 1 | make the **warm sliced peaches with peach sorbet** |
| step | 2 | assemble the **spinach, radicchio, and orange salad** |
| step | 3 | prepare the **couscous with herbs** |
| step | 4 | cook the **pan-seared sea scallops** |
| step | 5 | **serve** |

### shopping list

Ripe peaches

Peach sorbet

Radicchio

Prewashed baby or flat-leaf spinach

Orange slices
(from the salad bar)

Red onion slices
(from the salad bar)

Flavored or plain couscous

Fresh parsley, mint, or cilantro

Fresh thyme

Sea scallops

### from your pantry

Butter

Brown sugar

Fennel seeds

Extra virgin olive oil

Sherry or red wine vinegar

Salt

Freshly ground black pepper

All-purpose flour

Ground cumin

Cayenne pepper

Dry white wine

## luckyforyou

There are any number of ready-to-serve salad blends available. Use an Italian or European blend here if time runs short.

*"Because they are special and often pricey, sea scallops make a wonderful party dish or special-occasion dinner."* —minutemeals' Chef Marge

## step 1

### make the warm sliced peaches with peach sorbet

- 2 large ripe peaches
- 1 tablespoon butter
- 2 tablespoons brown sugar
- 1 cup peach sorbet, for serving

1. Peel and slice the peaches

2. Melt the butter in a medium saucepan. Add the sliced peaches and sprinkle with the brown sugar. Pan roast, tossing gently until they begin to caramelize, about 6 minutes. Remove the pan from the heat and keep warm, partially covered.

## step 2

### assemble the spinach, radicchio, and orange salad

- 1 small head radicchio
- 1 teaspoon fennel seeds
- 2 tablespoons extra virgin olive oil
- 1 tablespoon sherry or red wine vinegar
- 1/4 teaspoon salt
- 5 ounces prewashed baby or flat-leaf spinach
- 1 cup orange slices
- 1/2 cup thin red onion slices

1. Tear the radicchio into bite-sized pieces. Crush the fennel seeds.

2. In a serving bowl, combine the olive oil, vinegar, fennel seeds, and salt. Add the spinach, radicchio, orange slices, and onion and toss.

## step 3

### prepare the couscous with herbs

- 2 cups water
- 1 box (5.7 ounces) couscous
- 2 tablespoons chopped fresh parsley, cilantro, or mint

1. Pour the water into a 1- to 2-quart saucepan, cover, and bring to a boil over high heat. Stir in the couscous. Cover and remove from the heat. Let stand for 5 minutes, until the water is absorbed.

2. Chop enough fresh parsley, cilantro, or mint to measure 2 tablespoons.

## step 4

### cook the pan-seared sea scallops

- 3 tablespoons all-purpose flour
- 1 teaspoon ground cumin
- 1 teaspoon chopped fresh thyme
- 1/2 teaspoon salt
- 1/4 teaspoon cayenne pepper, or to taste
- 1 pound sea scallops
- 1 tablespoon extra virgin olive oil
- 1 teaspoon butter
- 1/2 cup dry white wine

1. In a medium bowl, combine the flour, cumin, thyme, salt, and cayenne pepper. Add the sea scallops and toss to coat.

2. In a nonstick skillet large enough to hold the scallops in a single layer without crowding, heat the olive oil and butter over medium-high heat. Add the scallops in a single layer and cook until golden brown and cooked through, about 3 minutes per side. Remove and divide among 4 serving plates; keep warm.

3. Add the wine to the skillet, increase the heat to high, and boil until reduced by half, about 3 minutes. Spoon the pan sauce over the scallops.

## step 5

### serve

1. Divide the scallops.

2. Fluff the couscous with a fork, add the chopped herbs, and toss to combine. Add a serving of couscous to each of the dinner plates.

3. Grind fresh black pepper over the salad and place the bowl on the table.

4. When ready for dessert, divide the peach slices among 4 dessert bowls and top each serving with 1/4 cup of the peach sorbet.

**Pan-Seared Sea Scallops**
Single serving is 1/4 of the total menu
CALORIES 533; PROTEIN 18g; CARBS 80g;
TOTAL FAT 17g; SAT FAT 4g; CHOLESTEROL 29mg;
SODIUM 613mg; FIBER 6g
*28% of calories from fat*

# shrimp and asparagus stir-fry
## asian orzo
## watermelon cubes

## shopping list

Orzo

Chopped scallions
(from the salad bar)

Asparagus

Medium shrimp, peeled and
deveined

Fresh gingerroot

Watermelon cubes
(from the salad bar or
produce department)

## from your pantry

Salt

Toasted sesame oil

Red pepper flakes

Garlic

Canola oil

Dry white wine or fat-free
reduced-sodium chicken
broth

Lite soy sauce

Pepper

serves 4

## **before**youstart

Bring a large pot of water to a boil,
covered. Chill the watermelon.

step **1** prepare the **asian orzo**

step **2** cook the **shrimp and
asparagus stir-fry**

step **3** **serve**

## **heads**up

If you opt for dry white wine in the stir-fry (instead of chicken broth), use a decent quality drinking wine, not the product called "cooking wine." Most cooking wines include salt—one of the most popular national brands on supermarket shelves contains 1 teaspoon of salt (2400 milligrams) per 8 ounces wine.

*"You can make this stir-fry even when asparagus isn't in season.
Substitute small broccoli florets, snow peas, or green beans."*

—minutemeals' Chef Ruth

## step 1

### prepare the **asian orzo**

Salt

8 ounces orzo

1/3 cup chopped scallions

1 teaspoon toasted sesame oil

1/8 teaspoon crushed red pepper flakes, optional

**1.** Bring 4 quarts water to a boil in a large pot, covered, over high heat.

**2.** Add the salt and the orzo. Cook about 9 minutes or as directed on package, until pasta is just tender. Drain the orzo and return to pot. Stir in the scallions, sesame oil, and crushed red pepper flakes, if using. Cover and keep warm until ready to serve.

## step 2

### cook the **shrimp and asparagus stir-fry**

1 1/2 pounds asparagus (about 24 stalks)

1 pound peeled and deveined medium shrimp

2 garlic cloves, minced

1-inch piece fresh ginger, peeled

1 tablespoon canola oil

1/4 cup dry white wine or fat-free reduced-sodium chicken broth

1 tablespoon lite soy sauce

Pepper to taste

**1.** Trim the tough stems from the asparagus. Cut the stalks on an angle into 1-inch pieces. Set aside. Rinse the shrimp and dry well on paper towels. Mince the garlic. Grate the ginger.

**2.** Place the oil in a large heavy skillet over medium-high heat. Add the garlic and ginger and stir-fry until fragrant, about 30 seconds. Add the asparagus and cook, stirring often, about 3 minutes.

**3.** Add the shrimp and stir-fry about 3 minutes or until just pink throughout. Add the wine or chicken broth and soy sauce and cook, stirring, for 1 to 2 minutes or until asparagus is just crisp-tender. Season with pepper.

## step 3

### serve

**1.** Divide the orzo among 4 wide soup bowls or dinner plates.

**2.** Divide the shrimp and asparagus stir-fry over the orzo.

**3.** When ready for dessert, serve the chilled watermelon, about 1 cup per person.

---

**Shrimp and Asparagus Stir-Fry**
Single serving is 1/4 of total menu

CALORIES 412; PROTEIN 28g; CARBS 59g; TOTAL FAT 7g; SAT FAT 1g; CHOLESTEROL 161mg; SODIUM 501mg; FIBER 4g

*16% of calories from fat*

# provençal fish chowder

fennel and parsley salad
toasted french bread
raspberries with orange
yogurt

## shopping list

Red pepper slices
(from the salad bar)

Canned garlic-flavored diced
tomatoes

Boneless cod fillets

Fresh basil

French bread

Fennel

Curly parsley

Marinated pitted olives

Raspberries

Whipped orange cream
low-fat yogurt

## from your pantry

Garlic

Red wine or fat-free reduced-
sodium chicken broth

Herbes de Provence or dried
thyme

Red pepper flakes

Pepper

Rice vinegar

Dijon mustard

Olive oil

serves 4

### **before**youstart

Preheat the toaster to warm the bread.

**step 1** cook the **provençal fish chowder**

**step 2** toast the **french bread**

**step 3** assemble the **fennel and parsley salad**

**step 4** **serve**

## headsup

When preparing fish for chowder, you want to cut it into pieces large enough to withstand heat and stirring. Cut the fish too small and you'll end up with a pot full of flaked (and overcooked) fish. For the same reason, choose fillets from firm-textured fish like monkfish, halibut, or haddock. Thin fillets, like those from sole or flounder, will fall apart too easily.

*"This is my take on bouillabaisse, the Provençal chowder. Mine is far easier, but still evokes the South of France."*

—minutemeals' Chef Sarah

## step 1

### cook the **provençal fish chowder**

- 1 cup red pepper slices, diced
- 1 large garlic clove, crushed through a press
- 1 can (14$\frac{1}{2}$ ounces) garlic-flavored diced tomatoes
- $\frac{1}{4}$ cup red wine, chicken broth, or water
- $\frac{1}{2}$ teaspoon herbes de Provence or dried thyme
- $\frac{1}{8}$ teaspoon crushed red pepper flakes
- 1$\frac{1}{2}$ pounds boneless cod fillets, cut into 1$\frac{1}{2}$-inch chunks
- Pepper to taste
- 2 tablespoons chopped fresh basil, for serving

1. Dice the red pepper slices. Crush the garlic.

2. In a large saucepan or Dutch oven, combine the red pepper, garlic, tomatoes, red wine, herbes de Provence or thyme, and crushed red pepper. Cover and bring to a boil over high heat. Reduce the heat to low and simmer 5 minutes.

3. While the broth simmers, cut the cod into 1$\frac{1}{2}$ inch chunks. Season the broth with pepper and stir in the cod. Return the mixture to a boil, cover, and simmer 5 to 7 minutes, gently stirring once, or until the fish is opaque in the thickest part.

4. While the fish is cooking, chop enough basil to measure 2 tablespoons and set aside. Remove the chowder from the heat and keep warm.

## step 2

### toast the **french bread**

- 8 slices (1 ounce each) French bread

Toast the French bread slices in the toaster oven until crisp. Transfer to a bread basket, and cover loosely to keep warm.

## step 3

### assemble the **fennel and parsley salad**

- 1 fennel bulb, trimmed
- 1 cup curly parsley sprigs, chopped
- $\frac{1}{4}$ cup marinated pitted olives, chopped
- 2 tablespoons rice vinegar
- 2 teaspoons Dijon mustard
- 2 teaspoons olive oil
- Pepper to taste

1. Trim the fennel. Remove the tough outside layer. Quarter the fennel lengthwise and remove the center core. Thinly slice the fennel.

2. Chop the parsley and then chop the olives. In a medium bowl, whisk the vinegar, mustard, and olive oil. Season with pepper. Add the fennel, parsley, and olives. Toss to combine. Place the bowl on the table with 4 salad plates.

## step 4

### serve

1. Ladle the chowder into 4 soup bowls. Add the basil. Serve with the salad and the toasted French bread, 2 slices per person.

2. When ready for dessert, place $\frac{3}{4}$ cup raspberries in each of 4 dessert dishes. Spoon 2 ounces (half of a 4-ounce container) of orange yogurt over each, and serve.

---

**Provençal Fish Chowder**
Single serving is $\frac{1}{4}$ of the total menu

CALORIES 482; PROTEIN 38g; CARBS 64g; TOTAL FAT 10g; SAT FAT 1g; CHOLESTEROL 70mg; SODIUM 1128mg; FIBER 11g

*17% of calories from fat*

minute

quick

# pasta and grains

meals
& healthy

# pasta with sausage and zucchini

## spinach, artichoke, and mushroom salad

## caramel apples and grapes

**menu** **gameplan**

### shopping list

Elbow macaroni

Zucchini

Precooked chicken or turkey sausage

Canned diced tomatoes with basil, oregano and garlic

Jarred marinated artichoke hearts

Prewashed baby spinach

Apples

Caramel fat-free yogurt

### from the salad bar

Red or yellow pepper slices

Mushroom slices (or from the produce department)

Seedless red grapes

### from your pantry

Garlic

Olive oil

Freshly ground black pepper

Grated Parmesan cheese

Olive oil cooking spray

Red wine vinegar

serves 4

### beforeyoustart

Bring the water to a boil in a large pot, covered, over high heat to cook the pasta.

step **1** cook the **pasta with sausage and zucchini**

step **2** assemble the **spinach, artichoke, and mushroom salad**

step **3** assemble the **caramel apples and grapes**

step **4** **serve**

**headsup** If you like your sausage spicy but can't find hot chicken or turkey sausage, simply add a good amount of crushed red pepper flakes to the sauce.

*"You can double the sauce without doubling the sausage and the fat. Add a can of drained white beans, instead."*

—minutemeals' Chef Marge

## step 1

### cook the **pasta with sausage and zucchini**

**for the pasta**

4 quarts water

12 ounces elbow macaroni

**for the sauce**

2 cups red or yellow pepper slices, halved

1 large zucchini, halved lengthwise and sliced

2 garlic cloves, crushed through a press

2 teaspoons olive oil

8 ounces precooked chicken or turkey sausage links, thinly sliced

1 can (14$^1$/$_2$ ounces) diced tomatoes with garlic, basil, and oregano, undrained

Freshly ground black pepper to taste

8 teaspoons (2 tablespoons plus 2 teaspoons) grated Parmesan cheese

**1.** Cook the pasta: Pour the water into a large pot and cover. Bring to a boil over high heat. Add the pasta to the boiling water and cook according to package directions just until *al dente*. Scoop out and reserve $^1$/$_4$ cup pasta-cooking water. Drain the pasta in a colander and return to the pot. Cover to keep warm.

**2.** Make the sauce: Cut the red or yellow pepper slices in half. Trim the zucchini, cut it in half lengthwise, and slice. Crush the garlic through a garlic press.

**3.** Warm the oil in a large nonstick skillet over medium-high heat. Add the peppers to the skillet. Cook, stirring often, for 3 minutes. Add the garlic and zucchini, and cook, stirring often, for 2 minutes, or until the vegetables soften slightly. Stir in the sausage, the tomatoes and their juices, and the pepper. Bring to a boil; reduce the heat to medium, and simmer for 6 minutes to blend the flavors.

**5.** Add the sauce and the reserved cooking liquid to the macaroni. Toss to mix.

## step 2

### assemble the **spinach, artichoke, and mushroom salad**

1 jar (6 ounces) marinated artichoke hearts

2 tablespoons red wine vinegar

Freshly ground pepper to taste

1$^1$/$_2$ cups mushroom slices

$^1$/$_2$ of a 5-ounce bag prewashed baby spinach

**1.** Drain the marinade from the artichokes, reserving 1 tablespoon.

**2.** Combine the reserved marinade and the vinegar in a salad bowl. Season with pepper. Add the mushrooms and drained artichokes, and toss to combine. Place the spinach on top; do not toss. Set the salad on the table with 4 salad plates.

## step 3

### assemble the **caramel apples and grapes**

2 large apples, cored

1 cup red seedless grapes

2 containers (8 ounces each) caramel fat-free yogurt

**1.** Core the apples and cut into thin slices. Divide among 4 dessert dishes. Sprinkle evenly with the grapes.

**2.** Spoon the yogurt from the tops of the yogurt on top of the grapes, dividing evenly. Spoon the caramel sauce from the bottoms of the yogurt over and refrigerate until serving.

## step 4

### serve

**1.** Divide the pasta among 4 bowls and sprinkle each serving with 2 teaspoons of Parmesan cheese. Place on the table.

**2.** Toss the salad and place on the table. Serve on the salad plates with the pasta.

**3.** When ready for dessert, serve the apples and grapes.

---

**Pasta with Sausage and Zucchini**
Single serving is $^1$/$_4$ of the total menu

CALORIES 721; PROTEIN 32g; CARBS 118g; TOTAL FAT 17g; SAT FAT 5g; CHOLESTEROL 51mg; SODIUM 1169mg; FIBER 11g

*21% of calories from fat*

# pasta salad
## with ham and mango
### breadsticks
### crisp vegetables platter
### pineapple-strawberry smoothies

menu
gameplan

## shopping list

Medium pasta shells

Lemons (for juice)

Chunk of lean reduced-sodium ham

Large ripe tomato

Fresh tarragon

Mango cubes or slices (from the salad bar)

Kirby cucumbers

Red pepper

Yellow pepper

Belgian endive

Radishes, cleaned and trimmed (from the salad bar)

Canned crushed pineapple in juice

Banana

Frozen unsweetened strawberries

Unsalted breadsticks

## from your pantry

Honey-mustard

Reduced-sodium chicken broth

Extra virgin olive oil

Salt and pepper

Skim-plus milk

Sugar

serves 4

## beforeyoustart

Bring a large pot of water to a boil, covered, over high heat to cook the pasta.

| step | 1 | make the **pasta salad with ham and mango** |
| step | 2 | assemble the **crisp vegetables platter** |
| step | 3 | make the **pineapple-strawberry smoothies** |
| step | 4 | **serve** |

## luckyforyou

This pasta salad is a great make-ahead dish. To keep the pasta from absorbing too much dressing, make the dressing in a large serving bowl and layer the ingredients on top, in the order given in the recipe; do not toss. Refrigerate, covered, for up to 6 hours, and toss right before serving.

*"This pasta salad is slightly sweet, slightly salty, and slightly creamy. It's a refreshing change from classic mayonnaisey macaroni salad."*

—minutemeals' Chef Paul

### step 1
## make the **pasta salad with ham and mango**

- 12 ounces medium pasta shells
- 2 lemons
- 2 tablespoons honey-mustard
- 2 tablespoons chicken broth or water
- 1 tablespoon extra virgin olive oil
- 6-ounce chunk lean reduced-sodium ham, diced
- 1 large chopped tomato
- 1 tablespoon chopped fresh tarragon
- 1 1/2 cups mango cubes
- Salt and pepper to taste

**1.** Bring a large pot of water to a boil, covered, over high heat. Add the pasta shells and cook according to the package directions, omitting the salt. Drain the pasta in a colander, rinse under cold running water, and drain well.

**2.** Meanwhile, squeeze the lemons to get 2 tablespoons juice. Pour the lemon juice into a serving bowl. Add the mustard, chicken broth or water, and olive oil and whisk until well blended.

**3.** Dice the ham, chop the tomato, and snip enough tarragon to measure 1 tablespoon. Place the ham, tomato, tarragon, and mango on top of the dressing. Add the drained pasta and salt and pepper and toss to mix well.

### step 2
## assemble the **crisp vegetables platter**

- 2 Kirby cucumbers
- 1 each red and yellow pepper
- 1 Belgian endive
- 1 cup radishes

**1.** Trim the cucumbers, halve them, and cut each half into thick sticks or wedges. Halve and core the red and yellow peppers; cut into wedges. Trim the attached edge from the endive and separate into individual leaves. If necessary, rinse and trim the radishes.

**2.** Place the radishes in a small bowl of ice water. Place the bowl on a platter. Arrange the cucumber wedges, red and yellow pepper wedges, and endive leaves around the radishes. Place the platter on the table.

### step 3
## prepare the **pineapple-strawberry smoothies**

- 1 can (8 ounces) crushed pineapple in juice
- 1 cup skim-plus milk
- 2 tablespoons sugar
- 1 large banana
- 2 cups frozen unsweetened strawberries

Place the undrained pineapple, milk, sugar, banana, and strawberries in a blender container. Refrigerate until serving time.

### step 4
## serve

**1.** Place the breadsticks in a tall glass or basket. Divide the pasta salad among 4 dinner plates and serve with the crisp vegetables.

**2.** When ready for dessert, blend the fruit and milk for 1 minute or until smooth. Pour into 4 tall glasses and serve.

---

**Pasta Salad with Ham and Mango**
Single serving is 1/4 of the total menu with 1 unsalted breadstick per person
CALORIES 702; PROTEIN 28g; CARBS 126g; TOTAL FAT 12g; SAT FAT 3g; CHOLESTEROL 26mg; SODIUM 741mg; FIBER 10g
*19% of calories from fat*

# fettuccine
## with spinach, pine nuts, and raisins

### romaine and mushroom salad

### frozen yogurt with orange sauce

## menu
## gameplan

**shopping list**

Fresh spinach fettuccine

Prewashed spinach

Pine nuts

Shallot

Fat-free half-and-half

Prewashed romaine salad mix

Mushroom slices
(from the salad bar or produce department)

Vanilla fat-free frozen yogurt

Orange juice concentrate

**from your pantry**

Salt

Olive oil

Golden raisins

Freshly ground black pepper

Extra virgin olive oil

Red wine vinegar

serves 4

## beforeyoustart

Bring a large pot of water to a boil, covered. Remove the orange juice concentrate from the freezer.

step 1 make the **fettuccine with spinach, pine nuts, and raisins**

step 2 make the **romaine and mushroom salad**

step 3 **serve**

## luckyforyou
No need to dirty a pan or set up a steamer to cook the spinach for the pasta dish—it cooks when the hot pasta-cooking water is poured over it. If it is not completely wilted at that point, don't worry; it will finish cooking when stirred into the hot pasta sauce.

*"Contrast is the key to keeping food interesting. The pasta has creamy sauce, crunchy nuts, chewy raisins—an inspired combination."*

—minutemeals' Chef Wendy

## make the **fettuccine with spinach, pine nuts, and raisins**

4 quarts water

Salt

9 ounces fresh spinach fettuccine

1 package (10 ounces) prewashed spinach

3 tablespoons pine nuts

1 large shallot, chopped

1¹/₂ teaspoons olive oil

¹/₂ cup golden raisins

¹/₄ cup fat-free half-and-half

Freshly ground black pepper to taste

1. Bring the water to boil in a large pot, covered, over high heat. Add the salt. Add the pasta and cook according to the directions on the package.

2. Place the spinach in a colander. Drain the pasta into the colander.

3. Meanwhile, in a small skillet, toast the pine nuts over medium heat, stirring occasionally, for about 5 minutes or until golden. Tip onto a small plate. Chop the shallot.

3. In the pasta-cooking pot, heat the olive oil over medium heat. Add the shallot and cook, stirring, occasionally, until nearly softened, 2 minutes. Stir in the raisins and half-and-half. Cook for 2 minutes, or until heated through. Season with salt and pepper, stir in the pasta and spinach, and toss to mix well. Cover to keep warm.

## make the **romaine and mushroom salad**

1 package (10 ounces) prewashed romaine salad mix

1 cup mushroom slices

2 teaspoons extra virgin olive oil

2 teaspoons red wine vinegar

Salt and freshly ground black pepper to taste

Place the romaine mix and mushroom slices in a salad bowl. Add the oil, vinegar, salt, and pepper. Toss the salad and place it on the table with 4 salad plates.

## serve

1. Divide the fettuccine among 4 large bowls. Sprinkle some pine nuts over each serving, dividing evenly.

2. When ready for dessert, scoop ¹/₂ cup frozen yogurt into each of 4 small bowls and drizzle 2 teaspoons of orange juice concentrate over each.

---

**Fettuccine with Spinach, Pine Nuts, and Raisins**
**Single serving is ¹/₄ of the total menu**
CALORIES 483; PROTEIN 18g; CARBS 84g;
TOTAL FAT 12g; SAT FAT 2g; CHOLESTEROL 5mg;
SODIUM 550mg; FIBER 12g
*20% of calories of fat*

# pasta with tomatoes and basil

fruit juice spritzers

grated zucchini with parmesan

orange-ginger sorbet

menu
**gameplan**

## shopping list

Pasta shells

Grape tomatoes

Fresh basil

Lime

Cranberry juice

Lime seltzer

Zucchini

Orange sorbet

Crystallized ginger

## from your pantry

Salt

Garlic

Extra virgin olive oil

Balsamic vinegar

Red pepper flakes

Olive oil cooking spray

Freshly ground black pepper

Grated Parmesan cheese

serves 4

## **before**youstart

Bring a large pot of water to a boil over high heat, covered. Preheat the broiler for the zucchini.

step 1 make the **pasta with tomatoes and basil**

step 2 make the **fruit juice spritzers**

step 3 cook the **grated zucchini with parmesan**

step 4 **serve**

## heads**up**

Crystallized ginger is available in the spice section of groceries. It is also available packaged in larger quantities elsewhere in the grocery store—either in the baking section or produce. If you can, get it at an Asian market where it is a fraction of the grocery store price.

*"This pasta is light and fresh, almost like salad. In the summer, try it with diced locally grown tomatoes."*

—minutemeals' Chef Wendy

## step 1

### make the **pasta with tomatoes and basil**

**for the pasta**

4 quarts water

Salt

8 ounces medium pasta shells

**for the sauce**

1 pint grape tomatoes

3 garlic cloves or enough to equal 3 teaspoons minced

1/2 cup shredded fresh basil

1 tablespoon extra virgin olive oil

1 tablespoon balsamic vinegar

1/4 teaspoon crushed red pepper flakes

1. Cook the pasta: Bring the water to a boil in a large pot, covered, over high heat. Add the salt and the pasta. Cook the pasta according to the package directions until *al dente*. Drain in a colander.

2. While the pasta cooks, make the sauce: Halve the grape tomatoes. Smash the garlic with the flat side of a Chef's knife. (For a more pronounced garlic flavor, crush the cloves through a garlic press.) Stack and thinly slice the basil leaves. In a large serving bowl toss the tomatoes, garlic, basil, olive oil, vinegar, and crushed red pepper.

3. Add the hot drained pasta to the tomato mixture. Toss to mix well.

## step 2

### make the **fruit juice spritzers**

1 lime

2 cups chilled cranberry juice

2 cups chilled lime seltzer

Cut 4 wedges from the lime. Pour 1/2 cup cranberry juice into each of 4 tall ice-filled glasses. Top each with 1/2 cup seltzer. Add a lime wedge to each.

## step 3

### cook the **grated zucchini with parmesan**

2 medium zucchini, about 10 ounces each

Olive oil cooking spray

1/2 teaspoon each salt and freshly ground pepper

2 tablespoons grated Parmesan cheese

1. Preheat the broiler. Grate the zucchini in the food processor or on the large holes of a box grater. Spread the zucchini on a jelly-roll pan. Coat with olive oil spray and sprinkle with salt and pepper. Toss to evenly distribute seasoning.

2. Sprinkle the cheese on top of the zucchini. Broil 5 inches from the heat for 5 minutes, until the zucchini is tender and lightly browned. Use a spatula to transfer the zucchini to a serving plate and place on the table.

## step 4

### serve

1. Serve the fruit juice spritzers.

2. Place the pasta on the table. Serve with the zucchini.

3. When ready for dessert, scoop 1/2 cup servings of sorbet into bowls and sprinkle each with 1 teaspoon chopped crystallized ginger.

---

**Pasta with Tomatoes and Basil**
Single serving is 1/4 of the total menu
CALORIES 475; PROTEIN 12g; CARBS 96g;
TOTAL FAT 6g; SAT FAT 1g; CHOLESTEROL 3mg;
SODIUM 515mg; FIBER 5g
*11% of calories from fat*

# pasta with three-mushroom sauce

## arugula and spring green salad

## seeded semolina bread

## tiramisú

**menu gameplan**

### shopping list

Rotini or other short pasta

Shiitake mushrooms

Portobello mushrooms (stemmed and presliced, if available)

Cremini mushrooms (stemmed and presliced, if available)

Ripe tomatoes

Fat-free pound cake

Mocha latte low-fat yogurt, or other coffee-flavored low-fat yogurt

Prewashed stemmed arugula

Prewashed spring or baby greens

Seeded semolina bread

### from your pantry

Onion

Garlic

Extra virgin olive oil

Dry red wine

Dried marjoram

Salt and pepper

Grated Parmesan cheese (optional)

Sambuca or Kahlúa, or rum (optional)

Coffee

Unsweetened cocoa powder

Low-fat salad dressing, preferably balsamic dressing

serves 4

### beforeyoustart

Bring the water in a large pot, covered, to a boil over high heat to cook the pasta.

**step 1** make the **pasta with three-mushroom sauce**

**step 2** make the **tiramisú**

**step 3** assemble the **arugula and spring green salad**

**step 4** serve

### luckyforyou

Stonyfield Farms makes 6-ounce containers of organic low-fat yogurt in many flavors, including the mocha latte we use in the dessert here. If you can't find it, substitute Dannon coffee low-fat yogurt, which comes in 8-ounce containers.

*"I used some red wine in the mushroom sauce. If you don't cook with wine, use 1/2 cup reduced-sodium chicken broth."* —minutemeals' Chef Marge

## make the **pasta with three-mushroom sauce**

### for the pasta

3 quarts water

8 ounces rotini or other short pasta

### for the sauce

1 small onion, chopped

4 garlic cloves, chopped

1 box (3 1/2 ounces) shiitake mushrooms

3/4 pound portobello mushrooms

1 box (10 ounces) cremini mushrooms

2 cups chopped ripe tomatoes (4 medium tomatoes)

2 tablespoons extra virgin olive oil

1/2 cup dry red wine

1/2 teaspoon dried marjoram

1/2 teaspoon salt

1/4 teaspoon pepper

1/4 cup grated Parmesan cheese, for serving (optional)

1. Cook the pasta: Pour the water into a large pot, cover, and bring to a boil over high heat. Add the rotini, stir to separate, and cook according to the directions on the package, until *al dente*. Drain, return to the pot, and keep warm, covered.

2. Prepare the sauce: Chop the onion and finely chop the garlic. Stem the shiitakes, then clean and quarter the caps. Cut the portobello mushroom caps into 1/4- by 2-inch slices. Stem the cremini mush-rooms, and slice the caps. Chop the tomatoes to measure 2 cups.

3. In a large nonstick skillet, heat 1 tablespoon of the olive oil over medium heat until hot. Add the onion and garlic and cook, stirring, for 2 minutes, or until softened. Add all the mushrooms and cook, stirring, for 1 minute. Add the tomatoes and stir to combine. Add the red wine and cook, stirring, for 5 minutes.

4. Stir in the remaining tablespoon olive oil, the marjoram, salt, and pepper, and cook for 3 to 4 min-utes. Add the cooked rotini to the mushroom sauce and toss to com-bine and heat through, if necessary.

## make the **tiramisú**

8 ounces fat-free pound cake

1 tablespoon Sambuca or Kahlúa, or rum (optional)

1/4 cup strong cold coffee

2 containers (6 ounces each) Stonyfield mocha latte low-fat yogurt

1 teaspoon unsweetened cocoa powder.

Cut the pound cake into cubes and place in a bowl. If using liquor, stir it into the coffee. Drizzle the coffee over the pound cake, toss, and refrigerate until ready to serve dessert.

## assemble the **arugula and spring green salad**

2 ounces prewashed stemmed arugula

6 ounces prewashed spring or baby greens

3 tablespoons low-fat salad dressing, preferably balsamic dressing

In a salad bowl, combine the arugula with the spring or baby greens. Add the dressing and toss to coat. Place the bowl on the table.

## serve

1. Serve the pasta in 4 bowls with the Parmesan for sprinkling over the top, if desired. Serve with the semolina bread and the mixed green salad.

2. When ready for dessert, divide the pound cake cubes among 4 dessert dishes. Spoon half a container of yogurt on top of each and sift some of the cocoa powder over the yogurt. Serve immediately.

**Pasta with Three-Mushroom Sauce**
Single serving is 1/4 of the total menu
CALORIES 654; PROTEIN 24g; CARBS 116g;
TOTAL FAT 11g; SAT FAT 2g; CHOLESTEROL 3mg;
SODIUM 887mg; FIBER 9g

*14% of calories from fat*

# scallops fra diavolo

micro-steamed broccoli
and carrots

seasoned breadsticks

raspberry sorbet with
lemon-blueberries

**menu**
**game**plan

serves 4

## shopping list

Fresh blueberries

Lemon (for juice)

Raspberry sorbet

Vermicelli or angel hair pasta

Bay scallops

Fresh basil

Broccoli florets (from the
salad bar or the produce
department)

Shredded carrots (from the
salad bar or the produce
department)

Seasoned breadsticks

## from your pantry

Sugar

Ground cinnamon

Salt and pepper

Olive oil

Fat-free marinara or other
tomato-based pasta sauce

Red pepper flakes

Butter

Dried tarragon

## beforeyoustart

Bring the water to a boil in a large pot,
covered. Rinse the blueberries.

step **1** make the **raspberry
sorbet with lemon-
blueberries**

step **2** cook the **scallops
fra diavolo**

step **3** make the **micro-
steamed broccoli
and carrots**

step **4** **serve**

**heads**up We call for bay scallops here,
which are bite-sized and thus
don't need to be cut up before cooking. You can also use
the larger sea scallops and quarter them before cooking.

*"Fra diavolo means 'from the devil.' This sauce is mildly hot; increase the red pepper if you want it really devilish."*

—minutemeals' Chef Ruth

## step 1

### make the **raspberry sorbet with lemon-blueberries**

1 pint fresh blueberries, rinsed and picked over

1 teaspoon fresh lemon juice

1 teaspoon sugar

Pinch cinnamon

1 cup raspberry sorbet, for serving

Rinse the blueberries and discard any that are green or shriveled. In a medium bowl, toss the blueberries with the lemon juice, sugar, and cinnamon.

## step 2

### cook the **scallops fra diavolo**

**for the pasta**

4 quarts water

Salt

12 ounces vermicelli or angel hair pasta

**for the sauce**

12 ounces bay scallops

1 tablespoon olive oil

Pepper to taste

2 cups fat-free marinara or other prepared tomato-based pasta sauce

1/4 teaspoon crushed red pepper flakes

1/2 cup firmly packed fresh basil leaves, shredded, for serving

**1.** Make the pasta: Pour the water into a large pot, cover, and bring to a boil over high heat. Salt the water. Add the pasta, stirring to separate strands. Cook until pasta is *al dente*, about 5 minutes or as directed on package. Drain in a colander.

**2.** Make the sauce: Rinse the scallops and pat dry with paper towels. Heat the olive oil in a large nonstick skillet over medium heat. Add the scallops, season with pepper, and toss to coat with oil. Cook the scallops, turning often, until they are nearly opaque, about 2 minutes.

**3.** Add the marinara sauce to the scallops and bring just to a simmer. Add the red pepper flakes and season with salt. Remove pan from heat.

**4.** Finely shred the basil: Stack the leave, roll them loosely, and cut crosswise into ribbons.

## step 3

### make the **micro-steamed broccoli and carrots**

12 ounces broccoli florets

1/2 cup shredded carrots

3 tablespoons water

1 teaspoon butter

1/2 teaspoon dried tarragon

Salt and pepper to taste

**1.** Place the broccoli and carrots in a large microwave-safe dish. Sprinkle with the water. Cover with a lid or vented plastic wrap.

**2.** Microwave on High for 6 to 8 minutes, stirring halfway through cooking, until crisp-tender. Drain. Transfer the vegetables to a serving bowl, and toss with the butter. Sprinkle with the dried tarragon, season with salt and pepper, and toss again. Place the bowl on the table with 4 salad plates.

## step 4

### serve

**1.** Divide the pasta among 4 broad-rimmed soup or pasta bowls. Spoon the scallop sauce over the pasta, and scatter the shredded basil over each portion.

**2.** Divide the broccoli and carrots among the salad plates, and arrange 2 breadsticks on each plate.

**3.** When ready for dessert, toss the blueberries and divide them among 4 small bowls. Top each serving with 1/4 cup of the sorbet.

**Scallops Fra Diavolo**
Single serving is 1/4 of the total menu

CALORIES 680; PROTEIN 34g; CARBS 117g;
TOTAL FAT 8g; SAT FAT 2g; CHOLESTEROL 44mg;
SODIUM 964mg; FIBER 12g

*11% of calories from fat*

# pasta with smoked salmon

### chilled tomato juice with cucumber spears and lemon

### watercress salad with croutons

### ginger-orange strawberries

## menu
## gameplan

serves 4

## beforeyoustart

Bring a large pot of water to a boil, covered. Chill the tomato juice.

| step | 1 | make the **ginger-orange strawberries** |
|---|---|---|

| step | 2 | make the **pasta with smoked salmon** |
|---|---|---|

| step | 3 | make the **watercress salad with croutons** |
|---|---|---|

| step | 4 | **serve** |
|---|---|---|

## shopping list

Crystallized ginger

Prewashed and hulled strawberries (from the salad bar)

Linguine

Neufchâtel cheese

Chives

Sliced smoked salmon

Lemons (for juice and wedges)

Watercress

Fat-free croutons

Orange–poppy seed marinade (Emeril's)

Reduced-sodium tomato juice

Kirby cucumber

## from your pantry

Orange juice

Salt

Olive oil

Freshly ground black pepper

Hot pepper sauce, optional

## luckyforyou
Smoked salmon has an assertive flavor so you need just a bit to give a salty, smoky note to the pasta. Many supermarkets carry it presliced in a cryovac package, or you can get it hand-sliced from a deli.

*"For a vegetarian dish, omit the salmon and add lemon zest, Parmesan cheese, fresh dill, peas—any or all of them."*

—minutemeals' Chef Wendy

## step 1

### make the **ginger-orange strawberries**

2 tablespoons crystallized ginger

2 cups strawberries, prewashed and hulled

1 tablespoon orange juice

Coarsely chop the ginger. Slice the strawberries in half lengthwise. In a serving bowl, mix the ginger, strawberries, and orange juice.

## step 2

### make the **pasta with smoked salmon**

**for the pasta**

4 quarts water

Salt

8 ounces linguine

1 1/2 teaspoons olive oil

**for the sauce**

1/3 cup chopped chives

4 ounces Neufchâtel cheese

1 teaspoon lemon juice

2 ounces smoked salmon

**1.** Cook the pasta: Bring the water to a boil in a large pot, covered, over high heat. Add the salt. Add the pasta and cook pasta according to the directions on the package, until *al dente*. Scoop out and reserve 1 cup pasta-cooking water. Drain the pasta in a colander and toss with the olive oil.

**2.** Make the sauce: Finely chop the chives. Place the Neufchâtel cheese and the reserved pasta-cooking water in the pasta-cooking pot, and cook over medium heat, stirring, until the cheese is melted and smooth.

**3.** Squeeze 1 teaspoon of juice from the lemon. Stir the lemon juice into the cheese mixture. Return the linguine to the pot and stir in the chives. Remove from the heat.

**4.** Coarsely chop the salmon and sprinkle over pasta. Season with just a pinch of salt and a generous grinding of pepper.

## step 3

### make the **watercress salad with croutons**

1 bunch watercress

1/2 cup fat-free croutons

3 tablespoons orange–poppy seed marinade

Remove the tougher stems from the watercress, rinse, and spin dry. In a salad bowl toss the watercress with the croutons and the marinade. Place the salad on the table with 4 salad plates.

## step 4

### serve

**1.** Pour the chilled tomato juice into 4 short glasses. Trim the Kirby cucumber and cut into quarters lengthwise. Cut the lemon into wedges. Add a cucumber quarter and a lemon wedge to each glass. Pass the hot pepper sauce so diners can add their own as desired.

**2.** Divide the pasta among 4 bowls. Serve the pasta with the salad.

**3.** When ready for dessert, divide the strawberries among 4 dessert dishes and serve.

**Pasta with Smoked Salmon**
Single serving is 1/4 of the total menu
CALORIES 553; PROTEIN 19g; CARBS 80g;
TOTAL FAT 16g; SAT FAT 16g; CHOLESTEROL 24mg;
SODIUM 976mg; FIBER 6g

*27% of calories from fat*

# thai noodles
## with shrimp
### watercress salad
### tropical fruit with almond cookies

## shopping list

Watercress

Canned juice-packed tropical fruit

Shredded coconut

Banana

Almond breakfast cookies, such as Stella D'oro (8)

Flat rice noodles

Scallions

Oyster sauce

Medium shrimp, peeled and deveined

Fresh cilantro

Peanuts

## from your pantry

Sherry vinegar

Dijon mustard

Honey

Canola oil

Sesame oil

Pepper

Rice or white wine vinegar

Brown sugar

Vegetable oil

serves 4

## **before**youstart

Bring a large pot of water to a boil, covered, over high heat to cook the noodles.

step 1 make the **watercress salad**

step 2 prepare the **tropical fruit with almond cookies**

step 3 cook the **thai noodles with shrimp**

step 4 **serve**

## **heads**up
If the flat rice noodles (about 1/8 inch wide) are not available, look for finer rice noodles, called vermicelli. If you can't find these, you can substitute 12 ounces of fresh fettuccine.

*"Pad thai, my inspiration for the noodles, may contain chicken or scrambled egg instead of shrimp. Either is delicious."*

—minutemeals' Chef Paul

## step 1

### make the **watercress salad**

1 bunch watercress, thick stems removed

1½ tablespoons sherry vinegar

2 teaspoons Dijon mustard

1½ teaspoons honey

1½ teaspoons canola oil

½ teaspoon sesame oil

1. Rinse and spin-dry the watercress. Remove any very thick stems. Place the watercress in a bowl and refrigerate.

2. In a small jar with a tight-fitting lid, add the vinegar, mustard, honey, and canola and sesame oils. Season with pepper. Shake well.

## step 2

### prepare the **tropical fruit with almond cookies**

1 can (15 ounces) tropical fruit, packed in juice

2 tablespoons shredded coconut

1 banana

8 almond breakfast cookies, such as Stella D'oro (for serving)

Drain the fruit and place it in a medium bowl. Scatter the coconut on top.

## step 3

### cook the **thai noodles with shrimp**

**for the noodles**

4 quarts water

8 ounces flat rice noodles

**for the shrimp and sauce**

2 scallions

3 tablespoons oyster sauce

3 tablespoons rice or white wine vinegar

2 tablespoons packed light brown sugar

1 teaspoon vegetable oil

12 ounces medium shrimp, peeled and deveined

¼ cup chopped cilantro, including some stems

3 tablespoons chopped peanuts

1. Cook the noodles: Bring a large pot of water to a boil, covered, over high heat. Add the noodles to the boiling water and cook according to the directions on the package. Drain well in a colander.

2. Make the shrimp and sauce: While the noodles cook, thinly slice the scallions and place in a small bowl. Stir in the oyster sauce, rice vinegar, and brown sugar.

3. Place the oil in a large nonstick skillet over medium heat. Add the shrimp and stir-fry for 3 minutes or until pink and firm. Stir in the oyster sauce mixture and the drained noodles. Cook, stirring, until the noodles are evenly coated and hot. Stir in the cilantro.

## step 4

### serve

1. Toss the watercress salad and place it on the table.

2. Divide the noodles among 4 dinner plates and sprinkle each serving with some peanuts, dividing evenly. Serve with the salad.

3. When ready for dessert, slice the banana into the tropical fruit mixture and stir gently. Spoon the fruit salad into dessert dishes and serve with the almond cookies.

---

**Thai Noodles with Shrimp**
Single serving is ¼ of the total menu
CALORIES 612; PROTEIN 21g; CARBS 96g;
TOTAL FAT 18g; SAT FAT 3g; CHOLESTEROL 126mg;
SODIUM 1063mg; FIBER 5g

*25% of calories from fat*

# garlic-chive grits
## with corn and tomatillo topping
### iceberg shreds salad
### piña colada and berry parfaits

**menu gameplan**

serves 4

|  | | |
|---|---|---|
| step | 1 | cook the **garlic-chive grits** |
| step | 2 | make the **corn and tomatillo topping** |
| step | 3 | make the **iceberg shreds salad** |
| step | 4 | assemble the **piña colada and berry parfaits** |
| step | 5 | serve |

## shopping list
Chives

Quick cooking grits

Tomatillos, fresh or canned

Fresh cilantro

Canned white shoepeg corn

Iceberg lettuce shreds

Shredded red cabbage

Reduced-calorie Ranch dressing

Blueberries

Raspberries

Piña colada fat-free yogurt

### from the salad bar
Red pepper slices

Shredded carrots

## from your pantry
White onion slices

Garlic

Skim milk

Dried thyme

Salt

Freshly ground black pepper

Canola oil

Ground coriander

Dried oregano

Orange juice

Sugar

 Tomatillos aren't tomatoes at all, but relatives of the ground cherry. If you use fresh tomatillas, give them a good scrub after you remove the husk—the skin is filmed with a sticky substance. If you can't find fresh or canned tomatillos, substitute large green tomatoes. Canned tomatillos contain a significant amount of sodium.

*"The grits with tomatillos is a superb brunch dish, especially topped with fried eggs, diet permitting."*

—minutemeals' Chef David

## step 1

### cook the **garlic-chive grits**

1 clove garlic, chopped

1 bunch chives, chopped

2 cups water

1 cup skim milk

1/4 teaspoon dried thyme

1 cup quick-cooking grits

Salt and freshly ground black pepper to taste

1. Chop the garlic. Snip the chives

2. Place the garlic, water, milk, and thyme in a heavy medium saucepan over high heat. Cover and bring to a boil, watching carefully to make sure it doesn't boil over. Stir in the grits; cover, reduce the heat to low and simmer, stirring occasionally 6 to 8 minutes. Remove from the heat, stir in the chives, and season with salt and pepper.

## step 2

### make the **corn and tomatillo topping**

4 fresh tomatillos (about 8 ounces), or 1 can (11 ounces)

1/4 cup cilantro sprigs

1 can (7 ounces) white shoepeg corn

1 cup red pepper slices

2 teaspoons canola oil

1/4 teaspoon ground coriander

1/4 teaspoon dried oregano

Salt and freshly ground black pepper to taste

1. Remove the green husks from the tomatillos, if using fresh. Rinse the tomatillos and cut each into quarters. Coarsely chop the cilantro. Drain the corn and the canned tomatillos, if using. Coarsely chop the red pepper.

2. Heat the oil in a large nonstick skillet over medium-high heat. Add the red pepper, cover, and cook, stirring once, 2 minutes. Add the tomatillos, cover, and cook 2 minutes longer, until they start to soften. Stir in the corn and oregano, cover, and cook 1 minute or until heated through. Season with salt and pepper.

## step 3

### make the **iceberg shreds salad**

4 cups iceberg lettuce shreds

1/2 cup shredded carrots

1/2 cup shredded red cabbage

1/2 cup white onion slices

2 tablespoons reduced-calorie Ranch dressing

In a large salad bowl place the lettuce shreds, shredded carrot shredded cabbage, and sliced onion. Add the Ranch dressing, toss, and set the bowl on the table.

## step 4

### assemble the **piña colada and berry parfaits**

2 cups blueberries

1 cup raspberries

2 tablespoons orange juice

1 tablespoon sugar

2 containers (8 ounces each) piña colada fat-free yogurt

Place the blueberries, raspberries, orange juice, and sugar in a bowl. Toss and let stand until ready for dessert.

## step 5

### serve

1. Divide the grits among 4 dinner plates. Top each serving with 1/4 of the corn and tomatillo topping. Serve with the salad.

2. When ready for dessert, layer the yogurt and the berry mixture in 4 wine glasses, dividing evenly, and starting and finishing with the yogurt. Serve immediately.

Garlic-Chive Grits with Corn and Tomatillo Topping
Single serving is 1/4 of the total menu.
Analysis uses fresh tomatillos; canned contain added salt.

CALORIES 423; PROTEIN 14g; CARBS 81g; TOTAL FAT 6g; SAT FAT 1g; CHOLESTEROL 7mg; SODIUM 733mg; FIBER 9g

*13 % of calories from fat*

# cuban hominy
## and black-eyed peas
### sugar and spice roasted plantains
### tomato, orange, and parsley platter
### tropical fruit-juice bars

serves 4

## shopping list

Ripe plantains (or slightly under-ripe bananas)

Canned black-eyed peas

Canned hominy

Ripe tomatoes

Flat-leaf parsley

Tropical fruit-juice bars

### from the salad bar

Onion slices

Red and green pepper slices

Orange slices

## from your pantry

Cooking spray

Olive oil

Sugar

Ground cumin

Ground cayenne pepper

Salt

Garlic

Red wine vinegar

Dried oregano

Freshly ground black pepper

Red wine vinegar

## beforeyoustart

Preheat the oven to 450°F to roast the plantains.

step **1** make the **sugar and spice plantains**

step **2** cook the **cuban hominy and black-eyed peas**

step **3** make the **tomato, orange, and parsley platter**

step **4** **serve**

## headsup
Hominy is dried white or yellow corn from which the germ and hull have been removed. You may be more familiar with ground hominy, or grits. The hominy and black-eyed peas are delicious wrapped in flour tortillas with a bit of salsa.

*"This meal seems exotic, but I thought of it (and found the ingredients) while browsing the aisles of my supermarket."*

—minutemeals' Chef Dave

## step 1

### make the **sugar and spice plantains**

Cooking spray

2 ripe plantains, or 3 slightly under-ripe bananas

1 teaspoon olive oil

2 teaspoons sugar

1/2 teaspoon ground cumin

1/8 teaspoon ground cayenne pepper

Pinch salt

1. Preheat the oven to 450°F. Coat a baking sheet with cooking spray.

2. Peel the plantains and slice into 1/2-inch-thick rounds. Transfer to a medium bowl. Add the olive oil and mix to coat the plantain slices. Add the sugar, cumin, cayenne pepper, and a pinch of salt, and mix.

3. Arrange the spiced plantain slices on the prepared baking sheet and roast for 15 minutes, until plantains are tender. If using bananas, start checking for doneness after about 11 minutes.

## step 2

### cook the **hominy and black-eyed peas**

2 cloves garlic, chopped

1 can (15 1/2 ounces) black-eyed peas

2 teaspoons olive oil

1 cup onion slices

1 cup mixed red and green pepper slices

1 tablespoon red wine vinegar

2 teaspoons ground cumin

1 teaspoon dried oregano

1 can (15 ounces) hominy

1. Finely chop the garlic. Drain and rinse the black-eyed peas.

2. Heat the oil in a large heavy saucepan over medium-high heat. Add the garlic, and the onion and pepper slices and cook, stirring occasionally, 2 minutes, or until the vegetables start to soften. Add the vinegar, cumin, and oregano and cook 1 minute longer.

3. Stir in the hominy, including the liquid, and the black-eyed peas. Bring to a boil, reduce the heat to medium-low, cover, and cook, stirring occasionally, until the mixture is hot and the vegetables are tender, about 8 minutes.

## step 3

### make the **tomato, orange, and parsley platter**

2 medium tomatoes, sliced

2 cups orange slices

Salt and pepper to taste

2 teaspoons red wine vinegar

3 to 4 sprigs flat-leaf parsley

Slice the tomatoes. Alternate the tomato and orange slices on a serving platter, overlapping slightly. Season with salt and pepper. Drizzle the red wine vinegar over the tomato and orange slices. Tear the parsley leaves from the sprigs and scatter on top. Bring the platter to the table.

## step 4

### serve

1. Divide the hominy and black beans among 4 large bowls. Divide the spiced plantains among 4 dinner plates, and pass the sliced tomatoes and oranges.

2. When ready for dessert, serve the fruit-juice bars.

**Cuban Hominy and Black-Eyed Peas**
Single serving is 1/4 of the total menu.
Analysis uses Dole strawberry fruit juice bars.
CALORIES 640; PROTEIN 9g; CARBS 140g; TOTAL FAT 6g; SAT FAT 1g; CHOLESTEROL 0mg; SODIUM 910mg; FIBER 16g
*8% of calories from fat*

# creamy polenta
## with black beans

### italian salad with carrots and radishes

### bananas with brown sugar glaze

**menu**
**game**plan

serves 4

## shopping list

Instant polenta

Crumbled garlic- and herb-flavored feta cheese

Large tomato

Canned diced tomatoes with garlic and onion

Frozen diced green pepper

Canned black beans

Prewashed Italian salad mix

Shredded carrots (from the salad bar or the produce department)

Sliced radishes (from the salad bar)

Orange juice

Bananas

## from your pantry

Dried oregano

Pepper

Low-fat balsamic vinaigrette dressing

Brown sugar

Light rum or vanilla extract

## beforeyoustart

Bring the water to a boil in a medium saucepan, covered, over high heat to cook the polenta.

| step | 1 | cook the **creamy polenta with black beans** |
| step | 2 | while the polenta cooks, make the **salad** |
| step | 3 | prepare the **bananas with brown sugar glaze** |
| step | 4 | **serve** |

 Corn and beans are a natural pairing, which is why we serve the black beans over polenta, or cornmeal. To make the meal even easier, spoon the beans over squares of hot cornbread (which will add calories and fat) and sprinkle the feta cheese over the top.

*"I love to mix and match cuisines. Here I borrowed from Italian, Spanish, and Greek, and it works."*

—minutemeals' Chef Marge

## step 1

### cook the **creamy polenta with black beans**

**for the polenta**

5 cups water

1 cup instant polenta

1/2 cup crumbled garlic- and herb-flavored feta cheese

**for the black beans**

1 large tomato, coarsely chopped

1 can (14 1/2 ounces) diced tomatoes with garlic and onion

1 1/2 cups frozen diced green pepper

1 teaspoon dried oregano

1 can (15 ounces) black beans, drained and rinsed

1/4 teaspoon black pepper

1. Make the polenta: Bring the water to a boil in a medium saucepan, covered, over high heat. Slowly stir in the polenta, bring to a bare simmer and cook for 5 minutes, stirring occasionally until polenta is thickened and soft. Stir in the feta, cover and remove from the heat.

2. Make the black beans: Coarsely chop the tomato. Stir together the fresh and canned tomatoes, green pepper, and oregano in a large skillet over medium heat. Bring to a boil and cook 5 minutes.

3. Drain and rinse the black beans. Stir the beans and black pepper into the skillet and simmer, stirring occasionally, for 4 minutes or until beans are hot.

## step 2

### while the polenta cooks, make the **italian salad with carrots and radishes**

1 package (10 ounces) pre-washed Italian salad mix

1/2 cup shredded carrots

1/2 cup sliced radishes

1/4 cup low-fat balsamic vinaigrette dressing

Divide the greens among 4 salad bowls. Scatter carrots and radishes on top. Place the salads and the dressing on the table.

## step 3

### prepare the **bananas with brown sugar glaze**

2 tablespoons packed brown sugar

1 tablespoon pineapple or orange juice

2 teaspoons rum or 1/4 teaspoon rum or vanilla extract plus 1 1/2 teaspoons water or juice

3 large bananas

Place the brown sugar, juice, and rum or extract and water in a medium microwave-safe bowl. Microwave on High for 40 seconds, stirring after 20 seconds, until the mixture is bubbly and the sugar is dissolved.

## step 4

### serve

1. Spoon the polenta onto 4 plates and top with the black beans.

2. Serve the salads, letting diners drizzle the dressing on top.

3. When ready for dessert, peel the bananas and slice them into a medium bowl. Toss with the sugar glaze, divide between dessert dishes, and serve.

---

**Creamy Polenta with Black Beans**
Single serving is 1/4 of the total menu

CALORIES 514; PROTEIN 18g; CARBS 97g; TOTAL FAT 7g; SAT FAT 2g; CHOLESTEROL 9mg; SODIUM 906mg; FIBER 14g

*13% of calories from fat*

# brown rice
## with curried-coconut chickpeas

### minty cucumber yogurt salad

### melon wedges with lime and honey

## menu
## gameplan

serves 4

## shopping list

Sweet potato

Canned chickpeas

Canned diced tomatoes

Cilantro

Shredded coconut, sweetened or unsweetened

Green chile or jalapeño

Cucumber slices (from the salad bar)

Plain fat-free yogurt

Honeydew melon or cantaloupe (from the salad bar or produce department)

Limes

## from your pantry

10-minute boil-in-bag brown rice (Success 10 Minute Brown Rice)

Olive oil cooking spray

Curry powder

Coriander seeds or ground coriander

Salt

Dried mint

Freshly ground black pepper

Honey

## beforeyoustart

Bring a large pot of water to a boil, covered, over high heat to cook the rice.

step 1 cook the **brown rice**

step 2 cook the **curried-coconut chickpeas**

step 3 prepare the **minty cucumber yogurt salad**

step 4 **serve**

## headsup

You can substitute cubes of butternut or acorn squash for the sweet potato in the curry. Or, to save time, use precooked diced white potatoes, stirring them into the chickpea-tomato mixture after 5 minutes.

*"Don't keep the rice, chickpeas, and yogurt separated on your plate. Try to get a bit of each in every bite."*

—minutemeals' Chef Lisa

### step 1

## cook the **brown rice**

2 bags boil-in-bag 10 minute brown rice

Bring a large pot of water to a boil, covered, over high heat. Add the bags of rice, pressing to submerge, and boil for 10 minutes. Remove the bags from the water and drain.

### step 2

## cook the **curried-coconut chickpeas**

1 small (about 8 ounces) sweet potato

1 can (19 ounces) chickpeas, drained and rinsed

1 can (14 1/2 ounces) canned diced tomatoes, drained

Olive oil cooking spray

1/2 cup water, plus more as needed

1/2 cup loosely packed cilantro leaves

3 tablespoons sweetened or unsweetened shredded coconut

1 hot green chile or jalapeño, coarsely chopped

1 teaspoon curry powder

1 teaspoon whole coriander seeds or 1/4 ground coriander

1/2 teaspoon salt

1. Peel the sweet potato and cut into 1/2-inch chunks. Drain and rinse the chickpeas; drain the tomatoes.

2. Coat a large nonstick skillet with olive oil cooking spray and place over medium-high heat. Add the sweet potato, chickpeas, tomatoes, and 1/4 cup of the water. Cover and cook, stirring occasionally and adding water as needed, until the sweet potato is tender, about 10 minutes.

3. Meanwhile, in a blender or food processor, place the cilantro, coconut, chile, curry powder, coriander seeds or powder, salt, and the remaining 1/4 cup water. Process 2 to 3 minutes, until the spices are as finely ground and the paste as smooth as possible. (Avert your face when opening the blender; chile oils can be hot.)

4. Stir the cilantro-chile paste into the chickpeas and bring to a simmer. Cover and cook for 2 minutes to blend the flavors.

### step 3

## prepare the **minty cucumber yogurt salad**

3 cups cucumber slices

1/4 cup plain fat-free yogurt

1/2 teaspoon dried mint, crumbled

1/8 teaspoon salt

Freshly ground black pepper to taste

In a medium bowl, stir together the cucumber slices, yogurt, mint, salt, and a generous amount of pepper. Place the bowl on the table.

### step 4

## serve

1. Open the rice bags and transfer the rice to a serving bowl. Transfer the curried chickpeas to a serving bowl. Place the rice and chickpeas on the table and serve with the cucumber salad.

2. When ready for dessert, divide the melon among dessert plates. Cut the lime into wedges and place a wedge on each plate. Drizzle 1/2 tablespoon of honey over the melon and serve.

**Brown Rice with Curried Coconut Chickpeas**
Single serving is 1/4 of the total menu
CALORIES 533; PROTEIN 14g; CARBS 117g;
TOTAL FAT 5g; SAT FAT 2g; CHOLESTEROL 0mg;
SODIUM 699mg; FIBER 12g
*8% of calories from fat*

# moroccan quinoa pilaf

green and black bean salad
apricot and cherry compote

## shopping list

Quinoa blend (Seeds of Change)

Currants

Canned diced tomatoes

Cilantro

Green beans

Canned black beans

Shallot

Lime (for juice)

Matchstick-cut carrots (from the produce department)

Apricot halves in lite syrup (Delmonte Natural Select)

Dried cherries

Granola

## from your pantry

Extra virgin olive oil

Onion

Garlic

Ground cinnamon

Salt

Dijon mustard

Red wine vinegar

serves 4

## **before**youstart

Bring a large pot of water to a boil, covered, over high heat to cook the green beans and pasta.

step 1 make the **moroccan quinoa pilaf**

step 2 prepare the **green and black bean salad**

step 3 make the **apricot and cherry compote**

step 4 **serve**

## luckyforyou

Quinoa is the highest protein grain available, and the only one that contains all 8 essential amino acids. It is also lower in carbohydrates than many other grains. The brand we use here, Seeds of Change, does not have to rinsed before using—others do. If your supermarket does not carry quinoa, check your local health food store.

*"Combining a new ingredient with familiar flavorings is an easy way to create new dishes that your family will love."*

—minutemeals' Chef Hillary

## step 1

### make the **moroccan quinoa pilaf**

1 teaspoon olive oil

1/2 small onion, chopped

2 garlic cloves, minced

1 package (5.6 ounces) quinoa blend

2 cups water

1/4 cup currants

1/2 teaspoon ground cinnamon

One can (14 1/2 ounces) Italian-style diced tomatoes, drained

2 tablespoons chopped fresh cilantro

Salt

Freshly ground black pepper to taste

1. In a 2-quart saucepan warm the oil over high heat. Add the onion and garlic and cook, stirring often, for 2 minutes. Add the package of quinoa and cook, stirring, 1 minute longer.

2. Stir in the water, currants, and cinnamon and bring to a boil. Cover, reduce the heat to medium-low, and simmer for 12 minutes, or until most of the liquid has been absorbed. Stir in the diced tomatoes and cilantro, and season with salt and pepper. Cover to keep warm.

## step 2

### prepare the **green and black bean salad**

8 ounces green beans, trimmed, or 1 package (10 ounces) frozen cut green beans

Salt

1 can (15 to 16 ounces) black beans, rinsed and drained

1 shallot, thinly sliced

1 tablespoon lime juice

1 tablespoon extra virgin olive oil

1 tablespoon Dijon mustard

1/2 teaspoon red wine vinegar

1/8 teaspoon salt

Pepper to taste

1/2 cup matchstick-cut carrots

1. Bring 1/2 inch water to a boil in a large skillet, covered, over high heat. Trim the tips from the green beans, is using fresh. Add some salt and the green beans to the skillet and cook for 5 to 7 minutes, or until tender. Drain the green beans in a colander and rinse briefly under cold running water.

2. Drain and rinse the black beans. Slice the shallot. Squeeze 1 tablespoon of lime juice. In a salad bowl with a fork, mix the lime juice, olive oil, mustard, vinegar, and salt and pepper. Stir in the green beans, black beans, carrots, and shallots. Toss to mix well and set the bowl on the table.

## step 3

### make the **apricot and cherry compote**

1 jar (26 ounces) apricot halves

1/3 cup dried cherries

2 tablespoons granola

1. Drain the apricots halves, reserving 1/2 cup of the syrup. Place the apricot halves in a medium bowl.

2. Bring the reserved syrup to a boil in a medium saucepan over high heat. Add the cherries, remove from the heat, and cover.

## step 4

### serve

1. Divide the quinoa pilaf among 4 dinner plates and serve with the salad.

2. When ready for dessert, stir the cherries and their soaking syrup into the apricot halves. Divide the compote among 4 dessert dishes, and sprinkle the granola over the tops, dividing evenly.

**Moroccan Quinoa Pilaf**
Single serving is 1/4 of the total menu
CALORIES 482; PROTEIN 11g; CARBS 95g;
TOTAL FAT 7g; SAT FAT 1g; CHOLESTEROL 0mg;
SODIUM 1061mg; FIBER 12g
*13% of calories from fat*

# spanish-style quinoa

## roasted red peppers
## bananas with crème caramel yogurt

**menu** gameplan

serves 4

step **1** make the **roasted red peppers**

step **2** cook the **spanish-style quinoa**

step **3** **serve**

### shopping list

Red peppers
Goat cheese (optional)
Quinoa
Fresh parsley
Canned black beans
Slivered almonds
Orange segments
(from the salad bar)
Bananas
Crème caramel fat-free
yogurt

### from your pantry

Olive oil
Salt
Orange juice
Garlic
Dried oregano
Freshly ground black pepper

**headsup** Fantastic Foods and Ancient Harvest both sell quinoa that need to be rinsed under cold running water just once to remove the saponin, a very bitter and slightly sticky substance on the surface of the seeds.

*"I love the way this looks on the dinner plate: Red peppers, speckled pilaf. It's so pretty, and simple."*

—minutemeals' Chef Dave

## step 1

### make the **roasted red peppers**

3 medium red peppers

2 teaspoons olive oil

Salt to taste

2 tablespoons goat cheese, optional

1. Turn the oven to 400°F. Halve the peppers, remove the cores and seeds, and cut the peppers into squares.

2. Place the peppers in a large oven-proof skillet, preferably cast iron. Add the olive oil and salt and toss until the peppers are well coated. Roast the peppers, stirring occasionally, for 13 to 15 minutes, until tender and some peppers are charred. Transfer to a serving bowl and crumble the goat cheese over, if using.

## step 2

### cook the **spanish-style quinoa**

1$\frac{1}{2}$ cups quinoa

1$\frac{1}{2}$ cups plus 1 tablespoon water

1$\frac{1}{2}$ cups orange juice

$\frac{1}{4}$ cup parsley leaves

2 cloves garlic

1 can (15$\frac{1}{2}$ ounces) black beans, rinsed and drained

$\frac{1}{4}$ cup slivered almonds

Olive oil cooking spray

$\frac{1}{2}$ teaspoon dried oregano

1$\frac{1}{2}$ cups orange segments

Salt and freshly ground black pepper to taste

1. Rinse the quinoa in a small strainer under cold running water for 2 minutes; drain. In a 2-quart saucepan stir together the quinoa, 1$\frac{1}{2}$ cups water, and the orange juice. Bring to a boil over high heat, reduce the heat to medium-low, cover, and simmer until all the liquid is absorbed, 12 to 15 minutes.

2. While the quinoa cooks, chop the parsley and the garlic. Drain and rinse the black beans.

3. Place the almonds in a small non-stick skillet over medium-high heat. Cook, shaking the pan, until lightly toasted 2 to 3 minutes; transfer to a small bowl. Spray the skillet with olive oil cooking spray. Add the garlic and oregano and cook, stirring, for 2 minutes, until fragrant. Add the black beans and the remaining 1 tablespoon water; cook until heated through, about 2 minutes. Remove from the heat and transfer to a large bowl.

4. Fold in the quinoa, parsley, almonds and orange segments. Season with salt and pepper.

## step 3

### serve

1. Divide the Spanish-style quinoa among 4 dinner plates. Place a serving roasted red peppers on each plate.

2. When ready for dessert, slice 1 banana into each of 4 dessert dishes. Spoon half of a container of crème caramel yogurt over each, and serve.

---

**Spanish-Style Quinoa**
Single serving is $\frac{1}{4}$ of the total menu
CALORIES 540; PROTEIN 19g; CARBS 96g;
TOTAL FAT 11g; SAT FAT 1g; CHOLESTEROL 0mg;
SODIUM 511mg; FIBER 15g
*18% of calories from fat*

# spicy bulgur risotto
## eggplant "steaks" with herbs
## chewy french baguette
## green grapes and sour cream

## shopping list

Eggplants

Fresh herbs such as parsley, basil, and chives

Fine-milled, quick-cooking bulgur

Frozen baby peas

Seedless green grapes (from the salad bar)

Reduced-fat sour cream (not nonfat)

Chewy French baguette

## from your pantry

Olive oil cooking spray

Salt and pepper

Olive oil

Garlic

Tomato paste

Red pepper flakes

Brown sugar

serves 4

## **before**youstart

Bring the water to boil in a tea kettle, covered. Preheat the broiler.

step **1** broil the **eggplant "steaks" with herbs**

step **2** make the **spicy bulgur risotto**

step **3** blend the **green grapes and sour cream**

step **4** **serve**

## heads up

Check the label on the bulgur to be sure it's the quick-cook kind. Otherwise, the soaking alone can take 20 minutes. If you can't find quick-cooking bulgur, you can substitute couscous, which takes less than 10 minute to prepare.

*"Eggplants are meaty, like portobello mushrooms—which you could use here, too. The steaks give heft to this meatless meal."*

—minutemeals' Chef Sharon

## step 1

### broil the **eggplant "steaks" with herbs**

2 medium eggplants, each about 1 pound

Olive oil cooking spray

$1/8$ teaspoon each salt and pepper

2 tablespoons mixed chopped fresh herbs, such as parsley, basil, and chives

1. Preheat the broiler. Place a sheet of aluminum foil on the broiler-pan rack. Trim the eggplants and slice them lengthwise into $1/2$-inch thick "steaks."

2. Place the eggplant on the prepared broiler-pan rack. Spray with olive oil spray and season with some of the salt and pepper; turn over, and spray and season the other side.

3. Broil the eggplant 3 inches from the heat for 8 to 10 minutes, turning once, until tender and lightly browned. Transfer to a platter and sprinkle with the herbs.

## step 2

### make the **spicy bulgur risotto**

$2^1/2$ cups water

1 tablespoon olive oil

1 clove garlic

1 tablespoon tomato paste

$1/2$ teaspoon salt

1 cup fine-milled, quick-cooking bulgur

$1/2$ cup frozen baby peas

$1/4$ teaspoon crushed red pepper flakes, optional

1. Bring the water to a boil in a tea kettle over high heat. Heat the olive oil in a large nonstick skillet over medium heat. Using a garlic press, crush the clove of garlic into the oil and cook, stirring, for 1 minute.

2. Add the tomato paste and salt. Stir in the boiling water to dilute the tomato paste, then stir in the bulgur, peas, and red pepper flakes, if using. Cover, remove from the heat and let stand 5 minutes, or until bulgur is tender and water has been absorbed.

## step 3

### blend the **green grapes and sour cream**

1 pound seedless green grapes

1 cup reduced-fat sour cream

4 teaspoons packed brown sugar

1. Strip the grapes off their stems, rinse in a colander, and transfer to a medium bowl. Stir in the sour cream.

2. Divide the grape mixture into four dessert and place in the refrigerator until ready to serve.

## step 4

### serve

1. Fluff the bulgur risotto with a fork and divide it and the eggplant slices among 4 dinner plates.

2. Place the baguette on the table and let diners tear off pieces.

3. When ready for dessert, sprinkle 1 teaspoon of brown sugar over each serving of grapes and serve.

---

**Spicy Bulgur Risotto**
Single serving is $1/4$ of the total menu, with one 1-ounce piece of baguette per serving

CALORIES 541; PROTEIN 13g; CARBS 94g; TOTAL FAT 16g; SAT FAT 6g; CHOLESTEROL 31mg; SODIUM 610mg; FIBER 16g

*24% of calories from fat*

# cheddar and grilled sweet onion quesadillas

## vegetable and bean salad
## pineapple italian ice with fresh pineapple

### shopping list

Vidalia onion

Tomato

Pre-shredded reduced-fat Cheddar cheese

Fat-free flour tortillas (8-inch diameter)

Fat-free sour cream

Lime (for juice)

Canned pinto or black beans

Prewashed iceberg lettuce shreds

Pineapple Italian ice

### from the salad bar

Shredded carrots (or from the produce department)

Chopped scallion

Pineapple chunks (or from the produce department)

### from your pantry

Olive oil cooking spray

Salt

Freshly ground black pepper

Ground cumin

Unseasoned rice vinegar

Olive oil

Cayenne pepper

serves 4

## **before**youstart

Chill the fresh pineapple.

step **1** cook the **cheddar and grilled sweet onion quesadillas**

step **2** assemble the **vegetable and bean salad**

step **3** serve

## headsup
We used reduced-fat cheese here instead of nonfat, for 1 reason: The less fat the cheese has, the worse the melting quality. While reduced-fat cheese does not melt as well as full-fat, it's a better choice than nonfat—so you can have your cheese and eat it, too.

*"Eating healthy doesn't mean you have to give up your favorite foods. This meal certainly doesn't taste like diet food."*
—minutemeals' Chef Marge

## step 1
### cook the **cheddar and grilled sweet onion quesadillas**

Olive oil cooking spray

1 large Vidalia or other sweet onion, sliced

Salt and freshly ground black pepper to taste

1 ripe medium tomato, chopped

1 cup shredded reduced-fat Cheddar cheese

3/4 teaspoon ground cumin

4 fat-free flour tortillas (8-inch diameter)

1/4 cup fat-free sour cream

1 tablespoon lime juice

1. Spray a grill-pan or skillet with olive oil cooking spray and heat over medium heat. Halve and slice the onion.

2. Place the onion slices in the grill-pan and season with salt and pepper. Grill, turning occasionally, for 8 minutes, or until lightly grilled and tender.

3. Meanwhile, chop the tomato. Combine the tomato, Cheddar cheese, and cumin in a small bowl.

4. Place the tortillas on a work surface. Place half the onions on 1 half of 1 side of each tortilla. Sprinkle the cheese mixture on top of the onions, and fold the tortillas in half, pressing firmly.

5. Spray a nonstick skillet with olive oil cooking spray and heat over medium heat. Place 2 of the filled tortillas in the skillet and cook 2 minutes per side, until lightly browned and the cheese has melted. Transfer to a plate and repeat with the remaining tortillas. While the quesadillas cook, squeeze 1 tablespoon lime juice. Combine the lime juice and sour cream in a small bowl; stir until blended.

## step 2
### assemble the **vegetable and bean salad**

1 can (15 ounces) pinto or black beans, drained and rinsed

2 tablespoons rice vinegar

2 teaspoons olive oil

Pinch cayenne pepper

Pinch ground cumin

Salt and freshly ground pepper to taste

2 cups shredded iceberg lettuce

1 cup shredded carrots

1. Drain and rinse the pinto or black beans.

2. With a fork, mix the vinegar, olive oil, cayenne pepper, cumin, and salt and pepper in a salad bowl. Add the lettuce shreds, carrots, and pinto or black beans. Toss to mix and place the bowl on the table.

## step 3
### serve

1. Using a pizza wheel, cut each quesadilla into 3 or 4 wedges and transfer to a dinner plate. Serve with the bean salad and sour cream.

2. When ready for dessert, scoop 1/2 cup of pineapple ice into each of 4 dessert bowls and spoon 1/2 cup chilled pineapple around each. Serve immediately.

---

**Cheddar and Grilled Sweet Onion Quesadillas**
Single serving is 1/4 of the total menu
CALORIES 394; PROTEIN 16g; CARBS 69g;
TOTAL FAT 8g; SAT FAT 4g; CHOLESTEROL 17mg;
SODIUM 782mg; FIBER 7g

*17% of calories from fat*

# a

Adobo, orange, chicken, 42–43

Almond(s), store-bought, 94–95

    Baked Apricots, 20–21

    cookies, 116–17, 152–53

    Peaches with Angel Food Cake, 110–11

    in Spanish-Style Quinoa, 164–65

Aloha chicken, 1960s, 48–49

Amaretti, peach halves with, 4–5

Ambrosial Angel Food Cake, 28–29

Apple(s)

    caramel, and grapes, 138–39

    Chicken Waldorf Salad with grapes and, 2–3

    crisp, with honey, 26–27

    pork chops with onions and, 88–89

    with Praline Dip, 38–39

    sorbet, store-bought, 74–75

Applesauce

    and Cookies, store-bought, 98–99

    pear-, chicken cutlets with, 46–47

Apricot(s)

    almond baked, 20–21

    and Cherry Compote, 162–63

    dried, store-bought, 94–95

    sauce, turkey cutlets with, 58–59

Artichoke, spinach, and mushroom salad, 138–39

Arugula and Spring Green Salad, 146–47

Asian Orzo, 132–33

Asian Tofu Salad, 16–17

Asian vegetables, scallops and, 128–29

Asparagus, shrimp and, stir-fry, 132–33

Avocado

    corn, and tomato salad with smoked turkey, 4–5

    in Corn and Crab Salad in Chili-Tortillas, 10–11

# b

Baby Carrots with Fresh Dill, 106–7

Baguette, French, chewy, 166–67

Baked Potato Chips, 62–63

Balsamic vinegar

    -Flavored Ice Cream with Strawberries, 124–25

    minted, melon with, 74–75

    sweet, strawberries with, 112–13

Banana(s)

    broiled, with chocolate sorbet, 16–17

    with Brown Sugar Glaze, 158–59

    with Crème Caramel Yogurt, 164–65

    in Raspberry Coolers, 86–87

    in Tropical Fruit with Almond Cookies, 152–53

    with Yogurt and 'Nilla Wafers, 72–73

Barley, herbed, 66–67, 88–89

Basil

    broccoli-, slaw, 86–87

    green beans with, 96–97

    pasta with tomatoes and, 144–45

Basmati Rice with Currants, 94–95

BBQ TVP on Whole-Grain Buns, 98–99

Bean(s)

    black, and corn relish salad, 18–19

    black, corn, and tomato chowder, 32–33

    black, creamy polenta with, 158–59

    black, green beans and, Salad, 162–63

    black, in quinoa, 164–65

    green, beef and, stir-fry, 74–75

    green, and black bean salad, 162–63

    green, French-cut, 84–85

    green, garlicky, 70–71

    green, potato and, salad with buttermilk dressing, 98–99

    green, roasted, 82–83

    green, with basil, 96–97

    pinto or black, vegetables and, salad, 168–69

    pinto, rice with, 42–43

    red, ground turkey burritos with, 64–65

    white, chicken, and fennel stew, 38–39

Beef

    and chickpeas, curried, 72–73

    and Green Bean Stir-Fry, 74–75

    tenderloin, pepper-and-fennel beef tenderloin, 82–83

    flank, teriyaki, 78–79

    ground, Burgers Italiano, 70–71

    ground, curried, and chickpeas, 72–73

    ground, in Mexican Meatball Soup, 26–27

    London broil, 76–77

    sirloin tips, in Hungarian Goulash Soup, 26–27

    top round strips, spicy Thai, 80–81

Berries, fresh. *See also specific names*

    with ladyfingers, store-bought, 108–9

Biscotti, store-bought, 70–71

    chocolate, 2–3

    and Fresh or Dried Figs, 70–71

    watermelon and grape medley with, 6–7

Blackberry and Lemon Yogurt Parfaits, 120–21

Blueberry(ies)

    lemon-, raspberry sorbet with, 148–49

    lemon ice with, 32–33

    parfaits, 154–55

Boggs, Bill, tip from, ix

Boiled New Potatoes with Garlic and Parsley, 40–41

Boston Lettuce Salad, 32–33

Bread(s). *See also* Baguette; Rolls

    French, toasted, 134–35

    garlic, grilled country, 126–27

    pita, 90–91

    pita, warm, breads with cannellini butter, 14–15

    seeded semolina, 146–47

    seven-grain, toasted, 12–13

    seeded crisp, 124–25

    Wasa Crisp, 2–3

Breadsticks, 4–5, 6–7, 140–41, 148–49

    seasoned, 148–49

Broccoli

    -Basil Slaw, 86–87

    and carrots, micro-steamed, 148–49

    with Cheese Crumbs, 50–51

    Pepper, and Mushroom Toss, 54–55

    roasted garlic couscous with cherry tomatoes and, 58–59

    slaw, red cabbage and, mustardy, 62–63

    stir-fry mix, in Curried Chicken Noodle Soup, 22–23

    and Tofu Stir-Fry, 100–101

    in Vegetable Stir-Fry, 78–79

Broiled Bananas with Chocolate Sorbet, 16–17

Broiled Chicken Sausage, 54–55

Broiled Pineapple with Lime, 60–61

Bruschetta, tomato, 24–25

Brussels sprouts, caraway, 66–67

Bulgur pilaf, minted, 84–85

Bulgur risotto, spicy bulgur, 166–67

Burgers. *See also* BBQ TVP; Patties

    Italiano, 70–71

    turkey, Sonoma, 62–63

Burrito Fixins', 64–65

Burritos, ground turkey, with red beans, 64–65

Butter, cannellini, warm pita breads with, 14–15

Buttermilk dressing, potato and green bean salad with, 98–99

Buttermilk Mashed Potatoes, 96–97

# C

Cabbage. *See also* Burrito Fixins'; Iceberg Shreds Salad; Slaw

    in Burrito Fixins', 64–65

    in Iceberg Shreds Salad, 154–55

    Napa, in Scallops and Asian Vegetables, 128–29

    red, and broccoli slaw, mustardy, 62–63

    red, slaw, gingered, 52–53

Caesar salad, grilled salmon, 6–7

Cake

    angel food, almond peaches with, 110–11

    angel food, ambrosial, 28–29

    angel food, with chocolate-espresso sauce, 46–47

    pound, orange-topped, 118–19

    pound, in Tiramisú, 146–47

    rice, mini, 16–17

Cannellini butter, warm pita breads with, 14–15

Cantaloupe

    in Caribbean Shrimp Salad with Curried Pineapple Dressing, 8–9

    in Melon Wedges with Lime and Honey, 160–61

    in Melon with Minted Balsamic Vinegar, 74–75

    in Spiced Melon Salad, 100–101

Capers, mustards, and fennel seed, flounder fillets with 106–7

Caramel Apples and Grapes, 138–39

Caramel Pudding, 106–7

Caramel-Drizzled Pineapple, 128–29

Caraway Brussels Sprouts, 66–67

Caribbean Pork Tenderloin with Peach Salsa, 84–85

Caribbean Shrimp Salad with Curried Pineapple Dressing, 8–9

Carrot(s)

    in Asian Tofu Salad, 16–17

    baby, with fresh dill, 106–7

    baby peas with ginger and, 116–17

    broccoli and, micro-steamed, 148–49

    in Boston Lettuce Salad, 32–33

    and Cilantro Salad, 20–21

    in Cucumber Raita, 72–73

    in Green and Black Bean Salad, 162–63

    in Iceberg Shreds Salad, 154–55

    Italian salad with radishes and, 158–59

    lemon-tarragon, 114–15

    micro-steamed sugar snap peas and, 46–47

    in Mixed Sautéed Vegetables, 122–23

    in Quick Vegetable Soup, 52–53

    Salad with Lime, 22–23

    in Vegetables and Bean Salad, 168–69

Cauliflower, micro-steamed, 118–19

Cheese

    blue, dressing, romaine salad with, 48–49

    Cheddar, and grilled sweet onion quesadillas, 168–69

    feta, in Creamy Polenta with Black Beans, 158–59

# Z